# ADMINISTRATIVE POLITICS
# AND SOCIAL CHANGE

St. Martin's Series
in American Politics

Stephen K. Bailey CONGRESS IN THE SEVENTIES
George Kateb POLITICAL THEORY
Grant McConnell THE MODERN PRESIDENCY
Ruth P. Morgan THE PRESIDENT AND CIVIL RIGHTS
Allan P. Sindler POLITICAL PARTIES IN THE
UNITED STATES
David G. Smith THE CONVENTION AND THE
CONSTITUTION

# ADMINISTRATIVE
# POLITICS
# AND
# SOCIAL CHANGE

*Louis C. Gawthrop*

ST. MARTIN'S PRESS • NEW YORK

To Nicholas

# *Preface*

---

This volume is designed, as are all of the books in this series, to provide the beginning college student of American politics with a broad view of a particular aspect of the American political process. The final impression that the book leaves with the reader is, of course, solely the responsibility of the author. In an effort of this type, possibly the best one can hope to achieve is to arouse the reader's interest to explore in depth the information and concepts that can be advanced here only in abbreviated form.

What emerges in the pages that follow is an extended essay on the role of administration in a period of rapid social change. Thus the scope of the subsequent chapters will extend beyond the narrow range of a simple description of public administration. Within the United States, the bulk of the administrative duties of the federal government are vested in the executive branch. The study of this aspect of government with a focus on its specific functions and technical details may be pursued in the advanced and specialized courses and programs of public administration. For the more eclectic reader who is concerned primarily about the relevance of democratic government in a turbulent world, this essay attempts to examine a particular segment of that government—the vast administrative domain of the federal executive branch—within the context of a single, dynamic society.

Administration is politics; and if politics is in fact simply a study of who gets what, when, and how, then executive-branch administrators—the bureaucrats—must be included as participants in the game of cutting up the pie along with Congressmen, Supreme Court Justices, party bosses, and lobbyists. Indeed, for the overwhelming majority of Americans the extent of their direct contact with "Washington" (or, for that matter with "City Hall") is limited to confrontations with governmental bureaucrats. Thus the political significance of administrative decisions, rules, regulations, plans, programs, opinions, attitudes, values, and actions or inactions cannot be ignored. The literature on the politics of administration is extensive, intensive, and, at least in one respect, culminal.

While one's understanding of the nature of the American political process remains transfixed to the concepts of pluralism, political bargaining, and the incremental allocation of resources, then the administrator must be understood as a political animal who must learn how to survive in an environment which is viewed as relatively stable, comfortably predictable, and, above all, highly politicized. This viewpoint has dominated the literature of public administration for the last thirty years, and virtually nothing can be added to what already has been recorded about the bureaucrat as a politically attuned operative.

During the past ten years, however, steadily mounting forces of technological, social, and political change have manifested themselves with an ever-increasing intensity. One immediate consequence of this development has been a fundamental change in the nature of the external sociopolitical environment of the bureaucrat. Less and less can the political behavior of a phantom public be taken for granted; instability has replaced stability, uncertainty has replaced predictability, and complex patterns of rapid change are becoming institutionalized. The shift from a stable to a turbulent environment has, of course, placed severe strain on all of our governmental systems and structures, but none have felt the strain more than has the administrative branch.

In a highly turbulent environment the function of the politically astute bureaucrat in the pluralist-bargaining-incremental system becomes increasingly vestigial. An evaluation of administrative politics caught up in a whirlpool of sociopolitical change thus can introduce to the beginning student a major alternative to the pluralist theory of democratic politics.

# Contents

# THE FEDERAL
# VINEYARD

In March 1966, less than six months after the membership of
the National Farm Workers' Association unanimously voted to strike
the grape growers of California, their leader, Cesar Chavez, appeared before U.S. Senator Harrison Williams' Subcommittee on
Migratory Labor. "All we need," spoke Chavez, "is the recognition
of our right to full and equal coverage under every law which
protects every other working man and woman in this country." A
simple request from a simple man pleading what appeared to him
to be a very simple cause. But below the surface of this scene of
simplicity the law frequently becomes a complex network as
snarled and tangled as the vines that bore the tender California
grapes. The law, too, has its many roots and branches, and the
complexity of the network that maintains the legal vineyard is com-
prehended only by those who work in the political and legal fields.
For the rest of the body politic—who generally prefer their law,
like their grapes, sweet, juicy, and simple to swallow—W. H. Auden
provides a more meaningful comment on the *corpus juris* than
Blackstone ever could:

> Law says the Judge as he looks down his nose,
> Speaking clearly and most severely;
> Law is as I've told you before,
> Law is as you know I suppose,
> Law is but let me explain it once more,
> Law is The Law.[1]

Nevertheless, a rich, full vineyard, legal or otherwise, does not spontaneously sprout forth in a blaze of glory. It requires patience, machinery, organization, and, most importantly, skilled workers. In the final analysis, it is the skilled administrators who breathe life into the law by application, direction, interpretation, and enforcement. It is these people who work together in an organized way to operate the machinery of government in a manner designed to yield efficiency, effectiveness, and equity. In short, it is the public bureaucratic system—composed of workers, techniques, and machinery—that is the essential supporting structure of our legal system.

In actual fact, of course, the bureaucratic support structure of the expansive federal government can hardly be portrayed in such ideally cohesive and integrated terms. Given a bureaucratic system involving eleven major departments and countless other semiautonomous and autonomous agencies and commissions, all of which require the full-time efforts of nearly 3 million civilian employees, coordination of function and integration of purpose frequently are lost in the emerging complexity.

For Chavez, who viewed the labor dispute between the grape workers and the owners in terms of social justice, that is, as right versus wrong, the function of the federal government was to provide unified, cohesive, coordinated guidance and assistance. "All we want from the government," he told the Williams Subcommittee, "is the machinery—some rules of the game." In short, Chavez sought an element of predictability, of consistency in the performance of the federal government which would permit his union to know the explicit procedural rules.

Unfortunately, Chavez was asking for something which our pluralist bureaucratic system is incapable of providing except in moments of national crisis. As will be seen in subsequent chapters, a high degree of predictability and consistency is, in fact, afforded to those groups and individuals in our society who recognize our political structure as a fragmented object that *reacts* in a disjointed, discontinuous manner rather than as one that *acts* in a unified, coordinated fashion. Those who expect a uniform set of rules to be implemented by a unified, integrated, and coordinated governmental structure entertain vain hopes. The vast bureaucratic network of the federal government is nominally held together by the President, who, acting as Chief Executive, is able to rely on some organizational theories, myths, rules, and regulations to obtain at least a semblance of unity. For the most part, however, the highly decentralized bureaucratic Leviathan exhibits a kaleidoscopic pattern in which the various subunits more frequently appear to be in business for themselves than to be working together for the same government. In this respect, the disjointed, conflicting, overlapping features of the federal bureaucracy are displayed in no case better than in the California grape strike.

**The Administrative Maze**

The fundamental dilemma confronting Chavez and all other farm-worker organizers before him is the simple political and legal fact of life that agricultural workers are excluded from the provisions of the National Labor Relations Act and hence do not come under the jurisdiction of the National Labor Relations Board (NLRB).[2] Specifically, this means that none of the enforcement powers of the NLRB which can be used to resolve labor disputes in the industrial segments of our society can be applied to disputes involving agricultural workers and employers.

This fact, of course, does not mean that farm workers are prohibited from organizing, or that any such organization may not bargain collectively with any employer or group of employers. It simply means that Chavez's United Farm Workers Organizing Committee (UFWOC), for example, unlike industrial labor organizations, has no recourse to the enforcement powers of the NLRB if the grape growers unilaterally refuse to bargain collectively with the UFWOC. From the beginning of the grape strike in 1965, the bulk of the California grape growers followed just this tactic of flat refusal to bargain collectively.

However, a major weapon of labor organizations—the strike—was available to the UFWOC, and Chavez built his whole campaign to bring the grape owners to the bargaining table around this relatively simple device. Grapes are highly perishable products. Any delay in the picking, packing, or distribution processes can result in significant financial losses for the owners. If the growers' labor supply could be choked off, then the grapes would never leave their vines, much less reach their markets. However, the immediate, short-term effectiveness of the strike by Chavez and his UFWOC members was seriously limited primarily because of various federal executive regulations and decisions.

From 1951 until 1964, the Mexican Farm Labor Act permitted the Secretary of Labor to authorize the importation of Mexican farm workers for temporary employment in the United States. Under this Act, the Secretary had to certify that U.S. workers were not willing, able, or qualified to meet existing farm labor needs, and that the importation of Mexican farm workers would not adversely affect the wage structure or working conditions of the U.S. labor market. In 1963, for example, the Labor Department announced that 186,900 Mexican farm workers were temporarily admitted into the U.S. under the provisions of the "bracero" program.

It was during the years of the operation of the bracero program that the most notorious and infamous abuses associated with temporary, transient farm workers became well publicized. The demise of the program finally came about in 1964, however, not as a result of an emergent social consciousness on the part of Congress, but rather, because of congressional realization that the mandated $1.40 per hour paid to the braceros was amounting to approximately $100 million dollars per year, virtually all of which was carried back into Mexico. Coming at a time when the nation was faced with a gold crisis, this was one drain that Congress could and did shut off. The bracero program formally died on 31 December 1964.

With this development, one might normally assume that the task of Cesar Chavez was made perceptibly easier. The Department of Labor could no longer authorize temporary importation of Mexican farm workers. The grape growers' steady supply of labor would be cut off. The only other labor supply was controlled by Chavez. An agreement between the owners and the UFWOC would have to be effected if financial ruin was to be averted. Such logic, however, was fanciful; the growers did have an alternative to the organized farm workers. Their alternative was again Mexican farm workers, brought into the U.S. not under a farm labor act but under the jurisdiction of the Justice Department's Immigration and Naturalization Service (INS).

Under the provisions of the Immigration and Naturalization Act of 1952 (McCarran Act) Mexican nationals may apply to become resident aliens in the U.S. Individuals whose applications are approved receive permanent alien registration cards which are commonly known as the "green card." These Mexican nationals may then enter and reside in the U.S. They may apply for U.S. citizenship after five years residence in the country. Many "green card" holders do in fact move to the U.S. (701,979 according to 1965 INS figures); many of these do indeed subsequently become U.S. citizens. A substantial number (47,315) of "green cards," however, are held by Mexican migrant farm workers who come into the U.S. to work and return to Mexico to live. "Green card" holders enjoy commuting privileges between the two nations that can be maintained indefinitely since the law does not require a resident alien to become a citizen.

In other words the bracero was simply replaced by the "green card commuter" as the main source of labor for the California grape growers, and as long as the procedure was maintained by the Immigration and Naturalization Service, Chavez's effectiveness in bringing pressure on the growers to bargain collectively was severely limited.

In July 1969 hearings were held by a House Education and Labor Subcommittee on a bill that would prohibit the employment of "green card" aliens as strike breakers during a labor dispute.[3] During the course of the hearings another major department of the federal government became involved in the discussion. The deputy assistant Secretary of State for Inter-American Affairs informed the committee that while the State Department was sympathetic to the objectives of the bill, international harmony between the U.S. and Mexico could be seriously disrupted if the provisions of the bill were enacted into law. Consequently, the commuting "green card" resident alien not only came directly under the jurisdiction of the Justice Department, but also found himself squarely within the sensitivity center of the Department of State. For these reasons, the chances of cutting off this rich supply of labor from the California grape growers disappeared.

The roles of the Departments of Labor, Justice, and State are significant as illustrations of federal bureaucratic overlap; but by no means do they exhaust the wide range of examples of bureaucratic overlap that could be cited in this case. For instance, both the strikers and the growers have benefited from various governmental programs that have provided resources of considerable value to each group. The Department of Agriculture's farm subsidy program, administered by the Agricultural Stabilization and Conservation Service, provided an important source of support for the major grape growers. Although grapes were not included in the farm subsidy program, the large conglomerate farm corporations (which had diversified holdings in wheat, corn, cotton, and feed grains—in addition to grapes) could collect substantial subsidies in these other crop areas, subsidies which could ease the losses incurred as a result of the grape strike. For instance, the major agricorporate conglomerate in the nation, the J.G. Boswell Company, represented one of the major grape producers in Southern California. In 1967, the Boswell Company received federal government subsidies totalling approximately $4 million. Other major grape growers who qualified under the program included the Kern County Land Company ($838,130), S.A. Camp Farms ($517,285), Giumarra Vineyard Corporation ($278,721), W.P. Camp and Sons ($238,816), and the Di Giorgio Fruit Corporation ($82,194).[4] The entire farm subsidy program was comprehensively revised by Congress in the Agricultural Act of 1970, which established a three-year price support program for wheat, wool, cotton, and feed grains. The most significant provision of the act was the $55,000 limit per crop that was imposed on subsidy payments for wheat, feed grains, and cotton only.

In addition to cash subsidies, the growers receive a substantial subsidy in the form of cheap water from the Bureau of Reclamation of the Department of the Interior. Over the years, the government has contributed approximately 75 per cent of the total cost of nearly $1000 per acre to irrigate the land in the Central Valley of California, including most of the grape-producing regions. For example, in 1960 Congress authorized the construction of the San Luis unit of the Central Valley project (which began in 1937). For the San Luis unit, a congressional appropriation of nearly $500 million was authorized. This appropriation was designed to irrigate a four-million-acre block of land, 13.8 per cent of which was owned by various large grape-producing farms, including the Kern County Land Company, Tejon Ranch, and Boston Ranch.[5] As the details of this situation became more widely known in subsequent years, the staid and traditional California State Grange was prompted to observe:

> The Grange was founded on the principles of law and order, and we hope the Federal Government will not openly encourage the permanent concentration of immense landholdings with the aid of federal funds which could freeze the great Central Valley of California into a pattern of huge landholdings, reminiscent of feudal Europe 150 years ago, or the present system of landholdings in Central and South America.[6]

Although certainly noᵗ of the same magnitude, federal assistance has also come to the striking workers, primarily in the form of funds from the Office of Economic Opportunity. For example, a $2 million OEO grant was used to establish a California Rural

Legal Assistance Program. Because of the rather unique circumstances surrounding the grape dispute, the Rural Legal Assistance program was especially helpful in defending migrant farm workers in motor vehicle cases. Without an automobile, farm workers were placed completely at the mercy of labor contractors who, alone, could provide the only other transportation to distantly removed grape fields. With an automobile, grape workers were able to retain a degree of independent mobility. The Rural Legal Assistance program was designed in large measure to protect the workers against arbitrary loss of that mobility.

A second OEO grant of $265,000 made directly to Chavez's UFWOC turned out to be more embarrassing than beneficial for the farm workers. Sargent Shriver, former Director of the OEO, announced the grant in 1966 as part of a program to begin community organization projects among the nation's poor. The only stipulation given to Chavez by Shriver was that none of the grant funds were to be used for strike purposes. Chavez gave the situation an honest appraisal and concluded that the UFWOC strike effort would inevitably become an integral part of any community organization project. Chavez demurred, and Shriver—under intense criticism from the growers and various California Congressmen—withdrew the grant.

Despite the governmental maze of bureaucratic apparatus, whose parts frequently operated at cross-purposes, Chavez and his farm workers were able to utilize their strike efforts effectively enough to obtain in June 1969, from ten major Coachella Valley growers an expression of willingness to negotiate. In this connection, both the UFWOC and the owners turned to still another government agency for assistance, the Federal Mediation and Conciliation Service. This agency enters into labor disputes when requested by all parties involved, and it attempts to provide expert guidance in the resolution of labor disputes.

The overwhelming majority of grape owners, however, were not prepared to follow the path taken by the ten Coachella Valley growers even though Chavez's organizing efforts, which had expanded into a nationwide sympathy boycott drive, were resulting in a major decline in the retail sales of table grapes. In August 1969 ninety-five major grape growers took advantage of the antitrust laws administered by the Federal Trade Commission and the Justice Department. They filed a $75 million damage suit in Federal District Court charging the farm workers with conspiring with retail grocer and butcher unions to keep grapes off the market.

Because of conflicting sets of data emanating from the Commerce Department, the Agriculture Department, various trade associations, and the labor unions, the exact effects of the national boycott were difficult to establish. Nevertheless, it seems clear that by 1969 backlogs of table grapes were building up substantially. At this point the Department of Defense entered into the situation by drastically increasing its purchase of table grapes, as Table 1 shows. Grape shipments to Vietnam alone quintupled from 468,000 pounds in fiscal year 1967 to 2.5 million pounds in fiscal year 1969.[7]

TABLE 1.  Department of Defense Purchases of Table Grapes

| Fiscal Year | Pounds (in millions) | Dollars (in millions) |
|---|---|---|
| 1966 | 7.5 | $1.04 |
| 1967 | 8.3 | 1.25 |
| 1968 | 6.9 | 1.32 |
| 1969 | 11.0 | 1.98 |

Understandably the farm workers were embittered by this development, the owners were delighted, and the Department of Defense was routinely casual. An official statement from the Department of Defense attempted to clarify its position:

> The Defense Department does not purchase grapes merely because they have been made more available and less expensive due to the effects of the boycott. Grape purchases are made by the Defense Supply Agency in response to requisitions from the military services. These requisitions are based on planned menus. . . . In the interests of objective and systematic management, menu planners (often working a year to 18 months in advance) should not be required to consider whether a labor dispute exists . . .[8]

The UFWOC strikers were no match for the Department of Defense. Obviously the increased purchase orders received from the military relieved the economic plight of the growers considerably. In an effort to regain the initiative in the labor dispute, the UFWOC moved in a new direction. Chavez charged that the growers' use of pesticides on their grape crops seriously imperiled the health of the farm workers, consumers, and wildlife. UFWOC workers took the position that the pesticides used contained active cancer-inducing ingredients. In support of this charge they offered the results of a Los Angeles County health study conducted in the area. This study reported that substantial quantities of grapes being sold in various retail stores contained pesticide residues that exceeded maximum levels established by the federal government. In addition, Chavez claimed that his workers who had been exposed to the pesticide residues developed a wide variety of ailments including eye irritations, rashes, dizziness, nausea, and double vision.

In response to these allegations Dr. Herbert Ley, Commissioner of the Health, Education, and Welfare Department's Food and Drug Administration, reported in September 1969 that exhaustive FDA tests of grapes in four major metropolitan areas, including New York City, revealed no pesticide residues in violation of federal health standards.[9] Other officials from HEW's Consumer Protection and Environmental Health Service, however, testifying before Walter Mondale's Senate Labor and Public Welfare Subcommittee on Migratory Labor, indicated that they were unable to produce any definitive data that would indicate that farm workers were adequately protected against harmful effects from the pesticides.[10] As the second session of the 91st Congress opened in January 1970, the issue of pesticide usage nationally became a subject of major legislative interest; but insofar as the grape strike specifically was concerned, the issue remained unresolved. Furthermore, on 30 April 1970 the chief pathologist of the FDA's Bureau of Science charged that middle-level administrators in the agency had expunged laboratory results, conclusions, and recommendations relating to food additives and pesticide safety to avoid weakening or contradicting established government policies in these areas. A subsequent investigation by a private consulting pathologist employed by the FDA generally confirmed the charge.[11]

The strike was finally broken in July 1970, a few weeks before the fifth anniversary of Chavez's "La Causa." On 29 July, after a week of quiet talks between Chavez and the largest, most intransigent growers from the Delano area, officials of the Giumarra Vineyard Corporation, the largest grape producer in California, signed a three-year contract with the UFWOC. By the first week in August, the union had signed similar contracts with approximately 75 per cent of all the state's growers. On 6 September the

Associated Press flashed a brief statement over its wires: "AFL-CIO President George Meany has notified all unions in the labor federation of the official end of the boycott of California table grapes."

Undoubtedly other federal administrative agencies were variously involved, either directly or indirectly, in this particular labor dispute. However, the illustration has been developed sufficiently to suggest that, given the nature of this conflict which involved a minimum of twelve different *federal* departments, agencies, commissions, bureaus, and services, the "rules of the game" which Chavez sought can hardly be stated in simple, straightforward terms.

## Politics or Administration?

The federal bureaucratic structure may quite properly be viewed as the administrative "muscle" of the President. Constitutionally, the President is charged with the responsibility to insure that the laws enacted by Congress are faithfully executed. As this responsibility has grown steadily since the start of the Republic, so also has the need to expand the scope and magnitude of the federal administrative structure. Three departments—State, War, and Treasury—were established by the first Congress. By the close of the 19th century, President William McKinley met with a Cabinet composed of eight departmental secretaries—State, War, Treasury, Navy, Post Office, Interior, Justice, and Agriculture. A Department of Commerce and Labor created in 1903 was subdivided into separate departments in 1913. Created in 1949 the Defense Department absorbed the Departments of War, Army, Navy, and the newly created (1947) Department of Air Force. The Department of Health, Education, and Welfare was established in 1953; and in 1965 and 1966 Congress established the Department of Housing and Urban Development and the Department of Transportation, respectively. In 1970 Congress passed—and President Nixon signed into law—the Postal Reorganization Act, which established the U.S. Postal Service as an independent agency of the federal government. The powers and duties of the Post Office Department were to be transferred to the new agency within one year following enactment. Thus in July 1971 the number of executive departments was reduced to eleven with the formal inauguration of the United States Postal Service. Add to this the equally steady growth of a wide variety of other administrative units including independent regulatory commissions, government corporations, and various agencies and offices, and one may begin to appreciate the vast complexity confronting every President as he enters office. In all, approximately 3 million persons in nonmilitary positions are currently employed by the government to insure that the laws passed by Congress are faithfully executed.

Its great size alone, however, does not explain the role that the administrative branch plays in the public policy process. As in the legislative and judicial branches of government, public policy decisions in the administrative branch are the result of interactions between individuals. The final policy outputs of any political system depend upon the inputs that are fed into the political process. In this respect, administrative inputs represent integral elements of the final public policy outputs, and it is essential that these inputs be clearly understood. For example, one could characterize the public policy process as it involves the judicial and legislative branches of government in terms of nine men, interacting in various ways, interpreting and evaluating the laws passed by the nation's 535 federal legislators. No one tries very hard any more to make the members of Congress appear in any context other than a political one. Political decisions are the lifeblood of the legislative process, and the conflicts which ultimately force their way into this arena are certain to be resolved by the time-honored political equation: negotiation plus compromise equals bargained agreements. Paul Diesing has stated the essence of the political decision-making process very clearly:

> *Non-political* decisions are reached by considering a problem in its own terms, and by evaluating proposals according to how well they solve the problem. The best available proposal should be accepted. . . . Compromise is always irrational; the rational procedure is to determine which proposal is the best, and to accept it. *In a political decision,* on the other hand, action is never based on the merits of a proposal but always on who makes it and who opposes it. . . . The best available proposal should never be accepted just because it is best. . . . Compromise is always a rational procedure, even when the compromise is between a good and bad proposal.[12]

The extent to which judicial behavior and the judicial decision-making process are characterized by political considerations is a thicket into which we need not venture. Suffice it to say that a considerable body of literature advances the notion that the most appropriate judicial stature, temperament, mind, and logic are characterized by a purely apolitical search for justice and equity.[13]

The question to be raised at this point is this: Between these two extremes of the highly and openly politicized legislative arena, and the purportedly detached, apolitical aloofness of the judicial chamber, where does one place the executive-branch administrator? Is he a "political animal" like his legislative counterpart, who thrives in the political environment; or is his style more apolitical, more judicious, impersonal, and professional? Since the beginning of our republic administrators have been ambivalent about what position along this hypothetical continuum they should assume. Given the nature of our political system, this ambivalence probably can never be completely resolved.[14]

Richard Harris provides an excellent (albeit somewhat imbalanced) insight into the extent of this ambivalence by contrasting the approaches to the administration of the Justice Department adopted by Attorney General John Mitchell and his Democratic predecessor, Ramsey Clark.[15] For Mitchell the dominant theme established throughout the Justice Department has been an unmistakable emphasis on the maintenance of law and order within the domestic sphere. In this context the administration of the Justice Department has clearly focused on operational efficiency. Clark, by contrast, set a departmental tone pitched high on social equity rather than internal operating efficiency or domestic tranquility. The major issues that consumed the attention of Clark and the department were the most volatile social and political crises of the day—civil rights, criminal rehabilitation, civil disobedience, and the right to dissent. For Harris, however, the contrast between the two men is much more subtle and paradoxical. Clark, in placing justice before order, was working toward the goal of developing the department into a "Ministry of Justice" which would insure the apolitical administration of fair and equitable law. Mitchell, on the other hand, in placing order before justice—in the name of apolitical, operating efficiency—has, according to Harris, directed the department into becoming a political force of the first magnitude.

One generalization that can be offered is that a clear dichotomy between absolute detachment from political factors and total political involvement is highly untenable. The manner in which the laws of the land are implemented becomes as important for a democratic polity as the manner in which the laws are passed or as the manner in which the values behind the laws are formulated. The sordid details of the Teapot Dome scandal involving, among others, President Harding's Secretary of the Interior, Albert B. Fall, provide an extreme example of how an administrative perspective of the public interest can be distorted by viewing the political world of government in one-dimensional terms.[16] But is the public interest not equally jeopardized by a comparably distorted, one-dimensional administrative perspective that focuses exclusively on operating efficiency? Certain segments of the American public at least, may view as totally insensitive the explanation of Defense Department officials in regard to the shipment of grapes to Vietnam that, "in the interests of objective and systematic management, menu planners (often working a year to eighteen months in advance) should not be required to consider whether a labor dispute exists. . . ."

The point is that the Congress of the United States is expected to assume an avowedly open political posture in our governmental system, while the Supreme Court is expected to assume a role which transcends the political emotions of the day. The real challenge for the administrator is to accommodate both attitudes by devising his own composite version of a sensible midpoint balance. But here, too, the danger is grave: in attempting to find the proper midpoint balance, a dead-center position may be obtained. The Leviathan may become the muscle-bound victim of administrative lethargy.

## The Ethos and Pathos of the American Political System

For nearly two centuries, American democracy has functioned without total interruption although, on occasion, it has functioned under severe stress. On the basis of this operating experience the best that can usually be said in its defense is that it works. As Kay Richards, the youngest member on the jury of the Chicago Seven conspiracy trial, noted in one of her posttrial articles, "The trial had to come to some kind of a conclusion," to prove that our legal system works. "It hurts people. But it works." [17]

Much the same, of course, can be said of our administrative system and the manner in which it dispenses justice and equity through its administrative channels. But the real question remains: How well does it work? How rational are public policy decisions reached by top-level executive officials? How comprehensive are the legislative review and evaluation of specific governmental programs? How effective is the implementation of public policy decisions by the executive bureaucracy? Unfortunately, all too often intuition and election returns have served as the only measures of administrative effectiveness. Despite efforts aimed at achieving a balanced administrative perspective, operating effectiveness is frequently defined in terms of political effectiveness; and, as Diesing noted,

political effectiveness is more often than not determined by a subjective value judgment—political desirability. In this connection,
Richart Neustadt has observed,

> . . . it is fair, I think, to say . . . that our public officers have
> been generally inclined to make the calculation without bother-
> ing their heads too much about their wherewithal in that if
> they could secure political assent, they could invent, or impro-
> vise, or somehow force the requisite responses from the men
> who actually would do the work, in government and out. The
> great machine of management would surely manage somehow,
> if the necessary sectors of the public, or the press, or Congress,
> or the Cabinet . . . were acquiescent.[18]

Thus to defend the present administrative system by declaring that
it works is a little like saying, "it is not irrational for an administrator to defend a policy as good without being able to specify
what it is good for."[19] The lack of concern for the consequences
of a particular administrative policy decision generates a shortsightedness which some view as a major defect in our governmental
process.

For others, however, the lack of attention given to the
long-term consequences of present acts is the real virtue of our
political system. An attempt to assess the future consequences of
administrative decisions—particularly of decisions about how scarce
public resources are to be allocated among the body politic—
would require a comprehensive degree of policy integration and
coordination which, many believe, would strip the American pluralist political tradition of its inherent vitality. From this perspective, the most important consideration in the allocative process,
given the nature of our pluralist political system, is seen to be the
maintenance of internal order and domestic stability.[20] Order and
stability can be maximized by maintaining a high level of consensual
agreement among the many heterogeneous groups in our society.
Such agreement is best achieved, it is argued, by fragmenting and
decentralizing the allocative decision-making processes. Conversely,
instability and disorder are bound to follow any effort at centralizing the process of allocation. Administrators are expected to work
within the pluralist framework by fashioning bargained agreements
among diverse interest groups, allocating political resources to each
group in the smallest increments that will resolve the conflicts implicit in the bargaining situation. The object, ideally, is to create a
"no-lose" solution for every conflict situation—that is, a solution
which leaves everyone directly involved satisfied, even if only mar-

ginally, and which leaves no one, directly or indirectly involved, totally dissatisfied. In the bargaining process, which involves negotiation, discussion, and compromise among the professional political actors directly involved, policy decisions that result in gross losses for any particular group, or set of groups, are inevitably ruled out. "The policies that survive are typically presented as benefiting everybody in a certain group, without affecting anyone outside it adversely." [21]

The limits placed on the decision-making capabilities of anyone who adopts this incremental allocative approach in our complex sociopolitical system will be examined in detail in Chapters Three and Four. For the moment it is enough to say that the incremental strategy permits political decision-makers to consider only those policies or programs that differ from existing policies or programs in small degrees. For example, the various administrative and legislative officials in the federal government, when confronted with demands stemming from the California grape strike for changes in public policy, responded in a clearly defined incremental manner. The allocation of OEO funds to establish a rural legal assistance program represented a small change in an existing program as did the Defense Department's grape procurement program. Braybrooke and Lindblom summarize their conclusions on incremental change quite specifically:

> To pursue incremental changes is to direct policy toward specific ills—the nature of which is continually being re-examined—rather than toward comprehensive reforms; it is also to pursue long-term changes through sequences of moves. Avoiding social cleavage along ideological lines, which is exacerbated when issues of ultimate principle are raised, incremental politics explores a continuing series of remedial moves on which some agreement can be developed even among members of opposing ideological camps.[22]

By limiting the scope of public policy debate to narrow increments of change, participants in any political conflict are supposedly capable of moving toward the resolution of conflict in a professionally detached, value-free manner. When confronted with two or more alternative programs, each representing an incremental change from an existing program, the decision-makers need only consider the extent to which the proposed alternative programs differ incrementally. A final choice is made possible by a preferential ranking of the incremental differences.

System stability thus becomes the ultimate goal of all who view the administrative process in these terms, and if one is satisfied that the future is defined by the present in terms of the past ("today's and tomorrow's problems are very much like yesterday's"[23]) then the necessity for comprehensive planning and centralized policy integration becomes politically irrelevant. Given the social changes now occurring within the United States, however, it may be argued that the no-lose solution for which the incrementalist strives has become a totally unrealistic expectation. Indeed, the usefulness of the incrementalist approach in what is increasingly becoming a *world* society may be called into serious question.

As Jack Walker points out in his critique of incrementalism,[24] the growing mood of cynical apathy among diverse disadvantaged groups in the nation can be safely ignored only so long by public officials who assume that silence means, at the very least, resigned concurrence. Chapters Three and Five will examine the techniques and sociopolitical consequences of the pluralist-bargaining-incremental process in detail, but Walker's point that, within the context of incrementalist theory, widespread public apathy is an essential prerequisite for democratic stability needs to be emphasized here.

To the extent that political apathy reflects a mild satisfaction with the manner in which political resources are allocated within the body politic, the relationship between apathy and stability can be viewed as functional. The relationship becomes potentially quite dysfunctional, however, to the extent that apathy simply covers over latent and growing frustration and anxiety. Frustration and anxiety must be considered in terms of their intensity and scope. The objective of the pluralist-bargaining-incremental system is to limit both the intensity and scope of latent frustration and anxiety. Failure to do so may create a highly complex and unstable set of interpersonal relationships within the body politic. Sociopolitical complexity is the bane of political stability. Confronted with a high degree of sociopolitical and technological complexity, the rationale of the pluralist-bargaining-incremental scheme is—as Walker contends—extremely difficult to maintain and the objective extremely difficult to accomplish.

At the present time, one is faced with a life and a world of unprecedented complexity. In part because of space-age developments in transportation and communication, the world has figuratively become one gigantic neighborhood—with all of the complexities associated with crowded neighborhood living. The world is just around the corner via TWA, or only as far away as your television set, whichever you prefer. But through continued technological developments in transportation and communications, new problems, new demands, new expectations, are bound to emerge in our world society. The pluralist-bargaining-incremental approach, which reflects a decidedly subnational orientation and assumes only limited, tightly contained, and localized conflict, can hardly be realistically applied in this situation of a shrinking, crowded world.

It is against this background of an emerging transnational world that the "dead center" position assigned to the executive branch by the pluralist-bargaining-incremental scheme must be considered. As will be discussed in detail in Chapter Three, the pluralist-bargaining-incremental approach provides its advocates with both an objective method and a subjective theory. First, it provides a method that can be applied to attain a satisfactory ("good enough") allocation of resources. Second, it provides the basis for a generalized, overall intellectual orientation which establishes its objective method as a positive subjective value for all social interaction. The present system undoubtedly works, but as the world closes in all around us it does not seem unreasonable to ask if a "good enough" performance is, indeed, any longer good enough. Our administrative system, continuing to operate from a point of maximum inertia, is—to borrow the 18th century English author Samuel Johnson's simile—"like a dog's walking on his hinder legs. It is not done well; but you are surprised to find it done at all." The extent to which the administration of American government and the making of decisions about the allocation of public goods are not well done—or surprisingly are done at all—will be examined in the following chapters.

## Chapter II

# THE
# ADMINISTRATIVE
# STRUCTURE

Every large, complex organization must be prepared to invest a certain amount of time, energy, and resources in the development and maintenance of an internal administrative structure. Organizational goals and objectives must be structured into meaningful programmatic operations; the organizational work force must be utilized intelligently and coordinated effectively; interpersonal relations must be directed to coincide with organizational goals and objectives; internal control patterns governing interpersonal relationships must be established to discourage dysfunctional behavior; organizational responsibility must be delegated in a clearly defined manner; and organizational authority must be maintained through the effective use of sanctions and rewards. In short, every large, complex organization must organize its personnel in a manner that is designed to insure the attainment of its goals in the most effective and efficient manner possible. The formal organizational patterns which result in this regard may be referred to as the organization's administrative structure.

Unfortunately, the analysis and description of administrative structures have assumed a certain static quality in the eyes of many students of administration. The building blocks of the organizational chart reveal the bones but hide the life of the structure. For many, the dynamic quality of organizations is to be found in the interpersonal relationships that develop within the organization, and most especially as these relationships unfold in connection with the organization's decision-making process. An extensive body of literature has emerged in the last twenty years which focuses on the description, analysis, and evaluation of organizational decision-making.

Despite the dynamic qualities assigned to the decision-making process and the static characterization of administrative structures, the central thesis of this chapter is that the administrative structure of the federal executive branch clearly influences the nature of the executive decision-making process. The pluralist-bargaining-incremental decision-making technique is viewed here as a major product of the executive administrative structure, and, as a consequence, the 'dynamic' state of the public policy process is very directly determined and controlled by the 'static' nature of the federal executive structure.

## The Hierarchical Structure

One way to emphasize this point, and to illustrate the rather unique context in which the public administrator is forced to operate is to contrast the executive bureaucratic structure to that of the classic bureaucratic model that is still fairly standard for most large-scale, private corporations. In large private corporations, every rational bureaucratic structure should be hierarchically arranged on the basis of graded authority. Figuratively speaking, this means the internal organization of authority in every bureaucratic structure—which, schematically, can be represented by a triangle —is arranged in a progression of greatest to least authority from the apex of the triangle to its base. An individual's authority in any such organization should increase as he moves away from the base and toward the apex of the triangle. By definition, therefore, the man at the top of the triangle should have more authority than anyone else in the organization. And a clearly defined chain of command should emerge connecting superiors and subordinates in a continuous series. Ultimate authority rests at the top of the triangle; those individuals who are situated on the first echelon below the apex are subordinate to the man at the top, but they are also superior to individuals who are situated on the next lower echelon. And so on down through the entire organization. Except for the individuals situated at the lowest level in the organization, virtually everyone else serves the dual function of being a superior and a subordinate.

The assumptions that control every superior-subordinate relationship are that superiors have the responsibility of reviewing and evaluating the actions and decisions of their subordinates, and, more importantly, they have the *authority* to criticize any actions or overrule any decision they consider detrimental to the best interests of the organization. Needless to say, the individual subordinate is expected to conform to any such overriding decisions made by his immediate superior. However, if one chooses *not* to conform willingly to the directives of superiors and their decisions, then the integrity of the entire organizational rationale has been challenged and threatened. Faced with such a challenge, the organization (in fact, higher echelon officials) must be prepared to invoke negative sanctions if internal order and control are to be maintained.

In this regard, the organization may impose a wide range of sanctions on the recalcitrant member—for example, transfer, loss of status symbols, censure, or demotion and the ultimate sanction of dismissal. In the fall of 1969, Henry Ford was not pleased with the way in which Semon (Bunkie) Knudsen, the President of Ford Motor Company, was running the corporation. Knudsen was summarily dismissed by Ford, who, according to one account, walked into Knudsen's office and curtly informed him, "You'll be leaving." President Nixon was not satisfied with the way in which his Director of the Interior Department's Bureau of Mines was carrying out his assigned responsibilities. Thus in March 1970 Nixon activated John F. O'Leary's resignation which had been routinely submitted in January 1969 when the new President assumed office.

In terms of organizational control, the centralization of power and authority contributes substantially to the maintenance of a closed, highly disciplined administrative structure. By contrast, an open-access, highly fragmented, decentralized administrative structure substantially weakens the formal superior-subordinate relationships. Henry Ford and Richard Nixon may appear to enjoy comparable grants of power and authority within their respective organizational settings; but, as noted above, the difference between an open and closed organizational structure can be dramatic. Henry Ford has built a bureaucratic citadel; the President of the United States sits atop a bureaucratic sieve.

## Constitutional and Historical Constraints

To appreciate governmental administrative structures, one must consider the historical tradition and the constitutional framework in which our political system has developed. The separation of powers concept, which represents a central feature of the U.S. Constitution, makes a very clear and explicit distinction between the three branches of government. The executive power shall be vested exclusively in the President, and it is the President, as Chief Executive, who shall insure that the laws of the land are faithfully implemented. Congress alone may pass the laws, the judicial branch may interpret the laws, but only the executive branch, directed by the President, can execute or administer the laws. In this respect, then, the Constitution places ultimate responsibility for the implementation of public policy directly in the hands of the President, and although this responsibility may be delegated by the President to subordinate executive officials, one might reasonably assume that all subordinates are directly accountable to the President. If this assumption were valid there would be no fundamental difference between the public and private versions of the closed, highly centralized bureaucratic structure. But all subordinate executive officials obviously are not directly accountable to the President. The spirit of administrative centralization implicit in the constitutional powers of the Presidency is effectively nullified by a second major feature of the Constitution—the concept of checks and balances.

The President may recommend public policy proposals, but only Congress may enact these proposals into public laws. The executive branch may administer the laws, but only the legislative branch can provide the resources necessary for administrative implementation. The President is solely responsible for insuring that the laws of the land are executed, but most of his top-level executive subordinates must be approved and confirmed by the Senate. All subordinate executive officials must be accountable to the President, but they also must be prepared to account directly (and annually) to various congressional committees. In short, if the separation of powers doctrine tends to make clear and precise distinctions between the authority and responsibilities of the three branches of government, the concept of checks and balances tends to blur that distinction, particularly in terms of executive-legislative relationships. In this context, the "separation" of powers has actually resulted in the diffusion of power, and in most instances of importance the two branches must move in harmony, if not in unison, if the public policy process is to advance.

This means, of course, that the *de facto* executive power of any President must be shared with an external group; that is, ultimate executive power and authority are not monopolized exclusively by the man at the apex of the bureaucratic triangle. Consequently all executive-branch administrators are constantly aware of the fact that they are subject to the directives of at least two masters. The divided loyalty that results from this circumstance brings with it many organizational problems, not the least of which is the fact that no President can ever safely take for granted the allegiance of his subordinates. Thus, despite the power explicitly conferred on the President by the Constitution, every President has had to exert a major effort simply to direct the bureaucratic structure that he supposedly is in charge of in the first place. Some Presidents have been successful in this regard and are recorded in history as the strong executives; most have not. In any event, the situation must be recognized as an intrinsic feature of our political system, and one which mitigates against the development of a highly centralized, tightly disciplined executive bureaucracy.

## The Limits of Executive Power

A second major factor which sets the federal executive structure clearly apart from the classical bureaucratic model and most corporate bureaucracies is the low degree of internal control that may be exerted over administrative personnel. Of the many politically appointed executive officials, one might expect that the President could maintain close contact and supervision over the members of his own Cabinet. In some instances, of course, a close relationship does develop. However, because of the complexity of the vast executive domain (to be discussed in detail later), the scarcity of time, the lack of full power and authority (as discussed above), and a built-in bureaucratic inertia, which is virtually impossible to overcome, it is quite unrealistic to expect the President to oversee effectively the operations of all eleven major departments. Each department, to a very real extent, must be viewed as a semi-autonomous administrative entity. The daily operating routines of each are, for the most part, firmly fixed by laws of long standing. Except when one of the departments may become embroiled in a crisis, the planning and supervision of normal operations of each must inevitably be delegated by the President to those individuals whom he selects as his departmental secretaries. In the face of a major national crisis in 1970, President Nixon became directly involved in the operations of the Post Office Department until the postal strike was resolved. President Kennedy closely followed the activities of the Justice Department during the civil rights crises of the early 1960s. All post-World War II Presidents have, virtually of necessity, been closely involved in the operations of the Departments of State, Defense, and Treasury. However, no modern-day President has been able to involve himself in the day-to-day operations of all executive departments, and the traditional semiautonomy of these executive units has become steadily reinforced in the current wake of mounting social, economic, and political complexities—foreign as well as domestic.

Regardless of how much conscious deliberation an incoming President gives to the selection of his departmental secretaries, each of them will inevitably become a "chief executive" in his own right. Insofar as presidential constraints are concerned, they are minimal; the President may serve as a prod, an inspirer, a coordinator, or an authority figure; as an overseer of daily operating procedures, however, the extent of his control is extremely limited. One important exception to this generalization applies when the President and one of his Cabinet or sub-Cabinet officials assume opposite policy positions. Under these circumstances, the President can invoke the ultimate sanction of dismissal (as Nixon indirectly did in the case of James Allen, Director of the Office of Education); but even this is a power which is generally used sparingly because of potential adverse political consequences. Instead the President can influence the daily operating procedures of the subordinate's administrative jurisdiction, strongly enough even to force the individual to resign his position. The constraints imposed on Robert Finch as Secretary of HEW by the Executive Office of the President were considerable and sufficient to obtain his "transfer." Additional White House checks against possible operational deviations purportedly were imposed on former Secretary of the Interior Walter Hickel. Where policy differences are minimal or completely absent, however, Cabinet and sub-Cabinet officials understandably enjoy a high degree of operating autonomy.

The image of these executive officials as private entrepreneurs should not be pushed too far. Admittedly free from all but the most modest constraints imposed from above, Cabinet and sub-Cabinet officials nevertheless inherit a structure which, for the most part, is extremely resistant to radical change and exceptionally slow in even modest adaptation. At best they inherit a relatively routine operation (Commerce, Labor, Interior) which has a long operating continuity and which yields a high degree of stability and permanence. Decades of repetitive operation cut deep tracks so that the wheels of the administrative structure are guided in a well-routinized manner. Occasionally, as was the case when former Postmaster General Winton M. Blount was faced with a nation-wide postal strike in March 1970, a temporary derailment may occur. But aside from such unpredictable blowups, these executive officials are just as much controlled as they are in control of their administrative domains. The more complex the department becomes, the more impossible it is for even the secretary to manage it directly. Thus for the Secretaries of State, Defense, and Health, Education, and Welfare, they, too, become heads of "mini-holding companies" which might be prodded, inspired, coordinated, but seldom controlled in any meaningful sense. Former Secretary of Defense Robert McNamara continues to represent the sole recent exception to this generalization.

In short, the President has limited control of his Cabinet and sub-Cabinet members; they in turn have limited control over the operations of their own subordinates. And yet, as suggested above, the administrative apparatus of the federal government continues to operate almost automatically. One explanation for this continuity can be found in the high degree of permanence that has been built into the structure as a result of the Civil Service Act of 1883.

The Civil Service Act created a dichotomy within the executive branch between career and noncareer administrators. As a result of this distinction, many students of government and public administration developed a parallel dichotomy in the early years of the 20th century between policy and administration.[1] The basic rationale of the civil service system was to afford security and protection against the capricious dismissal of persons in the executive structure who performed technical or purely mechanical functions in a totally apolitical manner. Such functions were viewed as falling within the scope of pure administration and, hence, were clearly distinguishable from functions directly related to the formulation of policy decisions. A theoretical dichotomy between policy and administration resulted: Responsibility for policy was assumed by noncareer appointees; responsibility for administration was assumed by career administrators—protected by the Civil Service Act. The fundamental assumption behind this rationale was that policy was politics but politics definitely did not include administration. The administrative functions of the executive branch were to be conducted by apolitical experts, be they typists or economists, whose functional responsibilities were totally insulated and isolated from the shifting political currents and eddies.

Nearly ninety years have passed since the "Pendleton" Act established the civil service system in the federal government, and countless studies, evaluations, amendments, and recommendations have been made concerning the operation of the system. On the basis of this extended experience with the civil service system, two highly confident generalizations can be made which are relevant for our present purposes. First, the dichotomy that the "Pendleton" Act sought to create between career and noncareer administrators has become a virtually immutable (and in some instances, debilitating) characteristic of the federal executive branch. Every incoming President must expect to inherit a vast army of career civil servants without whom the day-to-day operation of the federal government's administrative apparatus would grind to a halt. The career administrator provides invaluable continuity compared to the frequent and steady turnover among top-level policy executives. He provides the essential elements of stability and predictability— which are also the essential elements of the pluralist-bargaining-incremental tradition. Thus the dichotomy between career and noncareer officials has become an immutable and an *essential* feature of our fragmented executive structure.

The second generalization concerns the other dichotomy that the early administrative reformers saw as emerging between policy decisions and administrative decisions, that is, that policy decisions are political while administrative decisions are not. Again, after nearly ninety years of experience with the civil service system, the most charitable observation that can be made concerning this dichotomy is that it must be assigned a prominent position in the body of American political mythology. The distinction between policy and administration is most difficult to sustain in theory; in practice it is impossible. Despite the yeoman efforts of Woodrow Wilson, Luther Gulick, and other administrative scholars of the earlier period, their theoretical extrapolations always fell considerably short of the realities of administrative practice. Administration is politics in a very real and important sense. Given the nature of our pluralist political system there is virtually no such thing as a purely apolitical administrative decision. Any decision—save the most innocuous and trivial ones—made by an administrative official will almost inevitably run counter to the political objectives of some particular group in our society. As a consequence, the administrator—no matter how innocent, how objective, how disinterested, how apolitical he may attempt to be—creates political sound waves every time he makes an administrative decision. The statement by the Defense Department in connection with grape purchases was presented in the clearest, most explicit terms ("In the interest of objective and systematic management . . ."); nevertheless, the consequences of the decision were clearly political, at least insofar as the grape strikers were concerned. President Johnson's instructions to all executive departments and agencies in 1965 to adopt new planning-programming-budgeting techniques in the preparation of their annual budget requests could be viewed as simply an internal management directive aimed at modernizing those vital administrative functions.[2] For many individuals, however, his announcement was equal to a declaration of war in its purported intent to alter the political rules of the game that have traditionally governed the manner in which political resources have been allocated. One congressional subcommittee, in evaluating the presidential directive, drew the battle lines quite explicitly:

> If [the planning-programming-budgeting system] develops into a contest between experts and politicians, it will not be hard to pick the winners. They will be the politicians in the Congress and the White House.[3]

An intrinsic element of administration is politics. Administrative actions are integrally related to policy considerations, and administrative actions inevitably generate political consequences. This fact cannot be altered regardless of the nature of the administrative structure, the decision-making strategy, or the nature of the public policy process itself.

Ironically, despite the job security afforded by the Civil Service Act, the career administrator must perform his functions in a highly politicized environment; because of his civil service classification, however, he has become an important element in the pluralist-bargaining-incremental process. Working in this context, the career officials are afforded a wide range of opportunities to act as "free agents," so to speak. If the President is capable of exerting only limited control over his own appointed executive officials, his effective control over career civil servants virtually vanishes.

Except for behavioral infractions involving insubordination, gross inefficiency, criminal, subversive, or immoral activity, a career civil servant cannot be removed from his position unless the position itself is abolished. In instances of basic disagreements between superiors and subordinates involving interpretative, subjective judgments, virtually no way is open to separate the dissenting subordinate from the organization. This arrangement, of course, is completely consistent with the philosophical premises on which the entire civil service concept is based. Whether an individual career administrator agrees or disagrees with policy decisions is irrelevant; his only job is to administer policy made by others. Therefore his own public policy judgments have to be protected against capricious reprisals by his political superiors. Given this basic position, the chain-of-command concept in the classical bureaucratic model is broken, and one of the major factors that normally can be utilized to develop a strong sense of organizational loyalty is lost in the executive branch, at least insofar as career administrative officials are concerned.

Under these circumstances, it seems apparent that cohesiveness and administrative integration in the executive branch, if they are to occur at all, must be gained on the basis of a highly personalized approach by the President and his top-level policy executives. This is merely a restatement of the basic thesis set forth by Richard Neustadt that presidential power is, in fact, the power to persuade.[4] What is true of Presidents is true also of departmental secretaries and other top-level policy officials in the executive branch. All executive superiors have various resources at their disposal that can be utilized occasionally to gain support and cooperation from subordinate career administrators. The persuasive powers of the President and his Cabinet officials are somewhat like a radio signal being transmitted: the signal grows weaker as the distance from the transmitter increases, unless the transmitting power is increased. Unfortunately, as has already been noted, many limitations are imposed on the transmitting capacities of the President and his departmental secretaries.

For career administrators who are forced to "survive" in the pluralist political thicket, their "freedom," their insulation, their civil service security can, in fact, be the cause of extreme anxiety, frustration, and insecurity. For these individuals, a degree of psychological protection, security, and rewards must be found. In closed bureaucratic structures, the organization itself represents the only source of such rewards. Approved organizational behavior can be rewarded, protection can be provided, and individual security can be achieved. Within the open, fragmented, disjointed executive branch, however, career officials cannot confidently predict that "approved" behavior will yield a satisfactory flow of symbolic and material rewards aside from those mandated by the merit system; nor can they confidently assume that top-level executive officials will provide effective protection against external threats and challenges. In a word, the career civil servant is on his own, and in this connection it is important to note that his struggle for "survival" is significantly enhanced in one important respect. Unlike his counterpart in most private corporate structures, the public administrator is not immutably bound to a single chain-of-command pattern—other options are open, signals may be transmitted and received on other frequencies. The two main alternatives which are available to virtually every career civil servant are the congressional committees and the interest groups.

Interest groups represent logical, natural, and, usually, quite willing allies for career administrators. Nearly every executive unit, be it a department, agency, bureau, or office, has regular contacts with one or more private interest groups which are either directly or indirectly affected by the activities of the executive unit. The nature of this relationship may vary in every dimension, but the basis of the group process theory suggests that every private interest group is anxious to obtain any advantage it can in the public policy process. So obvious is this expected pattern of group behavior that frequently one loses sight of the fact that the process can also work in reverse—that is, an administrator may seek group support or "protection." [5] Threatened by the prospects of budget cuts, for example, an ambitious administrator may unofficially "lobby" his clientele groups to direct strong protests against any budgetary reductions to top-level executive officials, as well as interested legislators.

Much the same can be said of congressional committees. These legislative units are most popularly portrayed as the natural enemies of the administrator, and so often is this theme repeated that one, again, frequently loses sight of the fact that the relationship may be completely harmonious. For the harried congressman, a friendly administrator emerges as a valuable asset. The administrator becomes the source of necessary information as well as a vital source of action in terms of administrative decisions. Conversely, the congressional committees are quite willing, eager, and able to reciprocate in kind; the friendly administrator can expect favorable treatment from his committee, which means that, as with the interest groups, he can expect support and protection in times when support and protection might be needed.

The interest group and congressional committee alternatives open to the ambitious or ambivalent administrator need not be considered mutually exclusive alternatives. In effect, a four-cornered interaction pattern results between the individual administrator, the interest group, the congressional committees, and the policy executive to whom the administrator is nominally accountable, for example, the President, departmental secretary, or assistant secretary. The result, stated in simplistic terms, is that public policy decisions represent the consensus that emerges from a dominant coalition formed from these four elements. In actual practice, the interacting network becomes much more complicated; seldom is just one interest group involved in any policy or administrative conflict, and every administrative unit is accountable to at least four congressional committees—the authorization and appropriations committees of both the House and the Senate. In the final analysis, top-level executive officials (including the President) must frequently compete for the support and approval of influential and completely autonomous private interest groups and congressional committees in order to achieve their public policy objectives. More significantly, however, these top-level executive officials also must frequently compete for the support and approval of their own executive-branch subordinate officials—the career administrators— who, as a result of their semiautonomous status within the executive branch and their permanent tenure within the civil service system, frequently reveal a high degree of personal influence which can be effectively utilized to determine the outcome of political and administrative conflicts. As Richard Neustadt has pointed out most clearly, every President enters office as the nominal head of the executive branch, nothing more, nothing less. What he makes of his position after he assumes office will depend extensively on his own powers of persuasion. The executive apparatus is structured to respond to the forces of bargaining, negotiation, and compromise —in short, to the powers of persuasion. It is not geared to respond to the forces of direct commands from top-level executive officials, and least of all to direct commands from the President. The force of direct command can be effectively utilized only within those bureaucratic settings in which top-level officials have direct and exclusive control over the organizational futures of their subordinate administrative officials. The President's power in this regard is minimal at best. The "real" power of the office comes in the form of a blithe spirit which, unfortunately, eludes most occupants of the presidential office.[6]

## The Multitude of Organizational Entities

A third major factor that characterizes the difference between public and private bureaucracies and contributes significantly to the atrophy of executive-branch power and authority is simply the size, scope, and complexity of the executive domain. Technically it is the President who is responsible for insuring that the laws are faithfully executed, but in actual fact that becomes a moot responsibility, valid only in the abstract. Collectively, the size and scope of the eleven major departments virtually defy coordinated control. Individually, each represents a substantial operating entity, comparable in many respects to some of the nation's largest private corporations, if not some of the smaller nations of the world. For example, compared on the basis of the total number of persons (civilian) employed full time, a ranking of the (then) twelve executive departments and various corporations appearing on *Fortune* magazine's famed "500" list would result in the pairings in Table 2. Note that for the Defense Department's *civilian* personnel figure, the definition of "pairing" has to be slightly extended.

Viewed from another perspective the magnitude of the executive structure may be even more dramatically presented. In Table 3 the operating expenditures of the executive departments are contrasted to the total national government expenditures of selected nations. The latter figures represent conversions to U.S. dollars at free market rates, or approximations thereof. Given variable reliability of some original data sources, the table is presented for illustrative purposes only.

In addition to the eleven major departments, the President is also the nominal head of the vast array of independent commissions, corporations, agencies, offices, and boards that complete the total executive domain. Many of these units, such as the Migratory Bird Conservation Commission, Indian Arts and Crafts Board, Panama Canal Company (a government corporation), and the American Battle Monuments Commission, are insignificant insofar as their influence on broad public policy decisions is concerned. On the other hand, independent regulatory commissions such as the Federal Reserve Board, Interstate Commerce Commission, and the Securities and Exchange Commission, and government corporations such as the Tennessee Valley Authority, Federal Deposit Insurance Corporation, and Export-Import Bank enjoy great autonomy in making decisions which can seriously enhance or hinder the public policy objectives of the President. For years William McChesney Martin, former chairman of the Federal Reserve Board, viewed national banking policy from an entirely different perspective than did the fiscal and economic advisers of Presidents Truman, Eisenhower, Kennedy, and Johnson. Indeed, most of the independent regulatory commissions, designed to be immune from partisan politics, are quite independent of presidential direction and coordination; consequently they are often able to subvert in innumerable ways broad public policy initiatives of the President.

Possibly the best way to appreciate the overwhelming magni-

TABLE 2.  Comparative Ranking of Federal Executive Departments and Selected Private Corporations. Source: *Statistical Abstract of the United States, 1969* and *Fortune,* May 1970.

| Executive Department | Full-Time Civilian Employees | Full-Time Employees | Private Corporation |
|---|---|---|---|
| | | 436,414 | Ford Motor Company |
| | | 400,000 | General Electric |
| | | 258,662 | International Business Machines |
| | | 234,941 | Chrysler Corporation |
| Defense | 1,315,260 | 1,330,017 | Total of above four companies |
| Post Office | 720,810 | 735,856 | American Telephone & Telegraph |
| Health, Education and Welfare | 108,345 | 109,000 | Penn Central |
| Agriculture | 104,499 | 104,411 | Union Carbide |
| Treasury | 90,819 | 92,000 | F. W. Woolworth |
| Interior | 67,321 | 60,000 | Gulf Oil |
| Transportation | 59,931 | 63,898 | Trans World Airlines |
| State | 43,242 | 43,300 | Proctor & Gamble |
| Commerce | 35,927 | 37,073 | American Airlines |
| Justice | 35,457 | 36,000 | Allied Chemical |
| Housing and Urban Development | 14,022 | 14,682 | Pillsbury |
| Labor | 10,106 | 10,795 | Oscar Mayer |

tude of this many-headed leviathan that is the executive branch is to consider the various alternatives that the President may employ in an effort to implement effectively a particular public policy proposal. For instance, the President may attempt to reorganize various elements of the executive hierarchy to create the best possible fit between his policy goals and his supporting administrative apparatus. For example, he may become vitally concerned over

TABLE 3.  Comparative Ranking of Federal Executive Departments and Selected Nations. Source: Center for Comparative Political Research, State University of New York, Binghamton.

| Executive Department | 1967 Actual Budgetary Expenditure (in millions) | 1967 National Government Expenditure (in millions) | Nation |
|---|---|---|---|
| Defense | $68,776 | $63,981 | U.S.S.R. |
| Health, Education and Welfare | 35,153 | 38,520 | U.K. |
| Treasury | 13,098 | 14,188 | Japan |
| Agriculture | 5,828 | 6,225 | Australia |
| Transportation | 5,428 | 5,385 | Netherlands |
| Labor | 3,361 | 3,267 | Austria |
| Housing and Urban Development | 2,793 | 2,680 | Argentina |
| Post Office | 1,141 | 1,087 | Israel |
| Commerce | 738 | 741 | Colombia |
| Interior | 529 | 524 | Libya |
| State | 419 | 447 | Morocco |
| Justice | 409 | 340 | Zambia |

the procedures of federal law enforcement. He may feel that law enforcement requires his close supervision, even that the Federal Bureau of Investigation should be reorganized by transferring it from the Justice Department to the Executive Office of the President. The power to propose such a reorganization rests with the President; the power to disapprove a plan of reorganization rests exclusively with the Congress, and all reorganization plans of the President must be submitted simultaneously to both the House and Senate. The plan automatically becomes effective unless it is formally rejected by *either* house of Congress within sixty days of its submission by the President. (This power of Congress is referred to as the legislative veto power.) Thus the opponents of any reorganization plan have only to mobilize their resources in the congressional chamber where they can more easily defeat the proposal. If a President proposed to transfer the FBI to his Executive Office, he would inevitably meet strong opposition from a wide range of private interest groups and congressional committees that have assiduously developed close rapport with the Bureau over an extended period of time. No President would seriously consider such a move; no Congress would permit it.

Yet the reorganization authority is not an empty power granted to the President. In the four-cornered interacting network of President, administrators, interest groups and Congress, any effort by the President to break a strong alliance that may exist among the other three elements of the network is virtually doomed to failure. President Nixon received approval (that is, his proposal was not vetoed) to reorganize the Bureau of the Budget, an administrative unit which since 1939 has been viewed as the President's personal domain. In this case no strong external alliances were broken. Similarly, President Johnson was successful in obtaining congressional approval to reorganize two survivals of an earlier era which new technology had made obsolete: he abolished the Bureau of Locomotive Inspection; and he ended a tradition—almost as old as the nation itself—of awarding positions as customs collectors to political cronies by giving them to career administrators. In both instances, opposition to his proposals was minimal, and the reorganization plans were put into effect. It seems clear nevertheless that prospects of success are slight for any President who may attempt to achieve broad public policy objectives through a major administrative reorganization of the executive branch.

Faced with intense opposition, any presidential proposal for a major reorganization of any segment of the executive branch must go through the normal legislative process. Thus President Nixon's successful efforts in converting the Post Office Department into a government corporation came only after the proposal was passed in both the House and the Senate. The plan will fundamentally alter the Post Office Department, and so formidable were the defenders of its status quo, the enactment of the change probably would have been impossible ten years ago when President Kennedy assumed office. But in those ten years the efficiency and effectiveness of the department deteriorated dramatically. When Nixon assumed office in January 1969, the department and its defenders were caught between a strong sentiment in favor of a government corporation from the outgoing Democratic Postmaster General, Lawrence O'Brien, and a strong sentiment for modern management and administrative efficiency from the incoming Republican Postmaster General, Winton M. Blount. The nation's first postal strike in March 1970 hastened the reorganization drive. The executive proposal passed both houses of Congress with minimal difficulty, and the

President signed the bill into law on 12 August 1970. The new U.S. Postal Service went into formal operation on 1 July 1971.

The reorganization of the Post Office Department into a governmental corporation is illustrative of the point made at the outset of this chapter that the "dynamic" quality of organizations is inversely related to the "static" nature of their administrative structures. For all intents and purposes the structural relationships within the Post Office Department and between the Department and its relevant external environment (congressional committees, postal unions) had, over the years, become ossified. A rigid, inflexible structure inhibited dynamic interaction, and although the Nixon reorganization plan is no guarantee that a rejuvenated postal service will result, a structural reorganization was plainly a prerequisite for revitalization.

Much the same can be said of the attention being directed by President Nixon and his advisors toward a proposed reorganization of the entire federal departmental structure (see Figure 1). Regardless of the public policy pronouncements of any U.S. President today, his goals and programs must in fact be filtered through an administrative hierarchy that, for the most part, exhibits structural characteristics and managerial attitudes more in tune with a prior era. President Nixon's interest in reorganization is a recognition of this dilemma. By proposing reorganization he admits that administrative structure does make a policy difference.

Still in the planning stages, another report to President Nixon from his Advisory Council on Executive Organization proposes a complete overhaul of the independent regulatory commissions by converting them into agencies, each directed by a single administrator appointed by the President. All judicial functions formerly assumed by these commissions would be withdrawn and concentrated in a single administrative court. Even at this early stage it is possible to anticipate formidable opposition to this proposal if the President decides to present it to Congress for formal legislative enactment. The present influence patterns of many interest groups and congressional committees would be seriously altered by such a reorganization. Thus to accomplish this objective the President will certainly have to exert a major political effort. Unfortunately, engagement in conflicts involving major reorganization efforts can prove disastrous for substantive policy proposals—John F. Kennedy's proposal to establish a Department of Urban Affairs and Housing was decisively defeated. Many Chief Executives have rejected such direct, frontal assaults and have attempted instead to create new executive agencies that are charged with administering

Figure 1   **HOW THE PRESIDENT WOULD REORGANIZE THE CABINET**

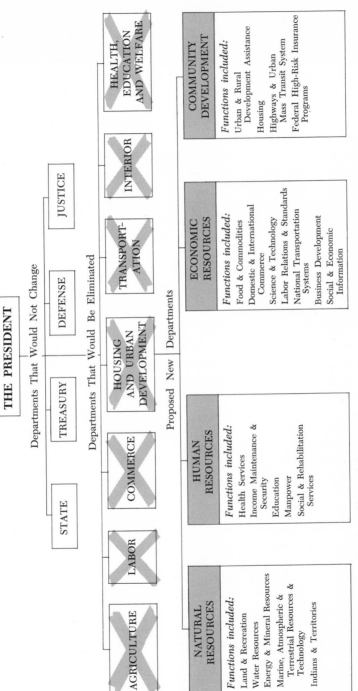

Source: *New York Times*, 28 March 1971. Used by permission

their assigned responsibilities in the manner desired by the President.

The creation of new units of the executive branch still requires congressional approval in the normal legislative manner—that is, it does not fall within the President's power of reorganization. But the advantages that the President may gain by creating new units can be considerable. This tactic is the most reliable way, for instance, to capture a fresh, innovative administrative spirit without eliminating any established, well-entrenched agency. New agencies initially create an exciting atmosphere in which imaginative experimentation frequently becomes an essential administrative practice. Operating flexibility is maximized and administrative inventiveness frequently flourishes. The old Economic Cooperation Administration (which administered the first U.S. foreign aid program), the Peace Corps, and the Office of Economic Opportunity are agencies which, when first established, proceeded in a highly innovative, experimental, and flexible fashion. In each instance, significant administrative achievements were registered on a short-term basis; the long-term achievements of each were probably less spectacular. The reasons for the short- and long-term differences are not complex.

Unfortunately, new agencies have a tendency to become old agencies as the passing of time dulls the luster and spirit of newness. Imaginative new programs gradually become routine, programmed activities. And as a consequence the executive structure is dotted with many agencies, boards, and commissions whose original thrust has expired but which continue to maintain themselves as administrative entities. For this reason the number of potential participants in any four-cornered conflict has increased steadily over the years as has the inclination of these participants to preserve the status quo aggressively.

Top-level policy officials, including the President, in an effort to improve administrative effectiveness in the public policy process, frequently adopt a third tactic—the advisory body. The advisory committee or commission can be utilized to gather information, evaluate given policy areas, and make recommendations concerning new policies. Several advantages are gained by the use of advisory commissions. First, if the members are carefully selected, the recommendations of the commissions may carry the weight of respectable and knowledgeable citizens whose credentials for political objectivity are impeccable. Second, commissions can help to build a consensus by mitigating opposition from legislative and interest group circles or by establishing countervailing support. Third, as already suggested, commissions are temporary; in theory, advisory commissions serve a short-run purpose by their intensive analysis of a specific topic and dissolve as soon as their missions are completed. Thus without disrupting any existing, permanent executive units, a study of high quality may be conducted without any commitment of permanent status to a new unit of the executive branch.

In actual fact, however, the "staying power" of even advisory commissions is nothing short of amazing. A General Accounting Office survey taken in the fall of 1969 revealed that there were 1,573 federal advisory committees, boards, commissions, councils, conferences, panels, task forces, and various other groups. Of the total number, 198 were identified as presidential advisory bodies. A senior consultant for the management consulting firm of Arthur D. Little, Inc. and a former assistant director of the Bureau of the Budget, William D. Carey, has stated:

> In my experience nothing was simpler than to set up an advisory group. It started wheels turning, it bought time, it was a surrogate for action, and it produced a kind of structural grandeur. It implied that somebody was taking care of a problem, and perhaps things would work out. This is the way of governments. I would point out, however, that the advisory committee system has its own laws of inertia and that there exists no satisfactory mechanism for ensuring its productivity or its accountability.[7]

In short, creating advisory groups simply adds more administrative units to the kaleidoscopic structure of the executive branch. The fragmentation of the policy-making function, regardless of how it may be disguised, is increased considerably as a result of this device. If Carey's analysis is correct, the pro-status quo, anti-innovative force within the executive branch is substantially strengthened by creating advisory groups—and the strategy of bargaining-incremental decision-making becomes all the more entrenched.

## A Fait Accompli

The tangled structure of the executive branch is certainly sufficient to bewilder even the most energetic and dedicated Chief Executive. Eleven major executive departments, countless agencies, commissions, and independent offices, plus 1500 advisory bodies create an irregular organization that virtually defies coordination of its activities. The consequences of this complexity are sometimes readily apparent. The farm workers involved in the California grape strike were the object of attention of twelve different agencies. Before the Environmental Protection Agency was established, administrative responsibility for control of environmental pollution was delegated to all executive departments except the Post Office and Labor Departments. Introduced by President Nixon as his Reorganization Plan No. 3 of 1970 and enacted into law on 2 October 1970, the Environmental Protection Agency was assigned many (but not all) of the major programs to combat pollution. Nevertheless, several units within the Executive Office of the President are involved in pollution control as are eight independent agencies, fourteen selected boards, four quasi-official bodies (National Academy of Sciences, National Academy of Engineering, National Research Council, and Environmental Studies Board), and, finally, the Environmental Policy Division of the Library of Congress. If the organization of public policy is examined geographically, then at least five major departments (Agriculture, Commerce, HEW, Interior, and Transportation) are involved in one way or another in the federal government's Appalachia program. If public policy is analyzed by who it serves, overlapping jurisdictions are again evident. For example, three departments (HEW, HUD, and Interior) share responsibilities for the welfare of the American Indian; and the Departments of HEW, Labor, Agriculture, as well as the Veterans Administration and other agencies, are all assigned various responsibilities concerning children.

The pattern of multiple and overlapping jurisdictions found throughout the executive branch makes administrative sense only insofar as centralized coordination by top-level officials insures against contrary policy outputs or unnecessary duplication of effort. Without such guidance and direction, this fragmentation of function and responsibility creates a multiplicity of little administrative fiefdoms. To develop an integrated approach to the general problem of urban and rural poverty, for example, all of the many administrative officials scattered throughout the executive branch who have been assigned responsibilities in this area must somehow be persuaded to join together and act in unison toward a unified policy goal. But in any group an individual may view cooperative, collective action with his potential "competitors" as a dangerous move. To retain one's sovereignty and entrepreneurial mobility is—given the nature of the political system—invariably wiser than to enter into "utopian" ventures based on collective and concerted action toward some long-range goal. Thus the structure creates a high degree of policy fragmentation and independent administrative behavior, which, in turn, place a high premium on bargained solutions, incrementally obtained. The bargaining-incremental strategy feeds back to reinforce the fragmented structure, and the cycle becomes virtually impossible to break at any point.

The structural indefiniteness so characteristic of the federal executive branch was actually (and deliberately) built into our political system at the Constitutional Convention of 1787. On the one hand, the firm commitment to a doctrine of a strict separation of powers was plainly written into the Constitution. The three branches of the federal government were clearly designed to be separate and coequal entities as a safeguard against the authoritarian exercise of power. On the other hand, the Madisonian doctrine of checks and balances provided political threads that bound the three branches together. With the passage of time the degree of fluctuation between these two doctrines has gradually diminished. At present the structural distinctiveness of the three branches, except for an occasional flare-up, must be viewed in conjunction with the high degree of functional integration that has developed, especially between the executive and legislative branches.

The checks and balances built into the structure at the outset of the republic have contributed to the reciprocal relationships that have developed between the executive and legislative branches. The establishment of a semiautonomous executive cadre of career administrators has created a structural impediment to coordinated, centralized executive activity. The proliferation of new agencies and advisory bodies out of efforts to circumvent the sluggishness inherent in the bureaucratic structure has compounded the problems of administrative supervision and accountability. Each of these factors has contributed significantly to the virtual institutionalization of the four-cornered conflict among president, administrators, interest groups, and Congress and the consequent fact that such conflict can only be effectively resolved through the application of a bargaining-incremental strategy. Therefore the public policy decisions ultimately agreed upon reflect the basic characteristics of the administrative structure in which they are formed—they are disjointed, fragmentary agreements upheld tenuously by temporary coalitions. Given the structure of the executive branch (and its important relationship to the structure of the legislative branch) the manner in which the bargaining-incremental strategy is developed, applied, and concluded in specific conflict situations is a matter of some importance, especially since public policy outputs are, in the main, products of this strategy. How four-corner conflicts are resolved in our political system and the role that executive-branch participants play in resolving them are the subjects of the next chapter.

---

## Chapter III

# THE STRATEGY
# OF GAMES

Years ago, newspaper reporter Frank Kent wrote a daily column under the banner, "The Great Game of Politics," which he later expanded and published in a book bearing the same title. For Kent, politics could be understood only if viewed in terms of a game played by an assortment of professional politicians, each of whom sought to end up winning more than he lost.

> . . . the thing that gets [the professional politician] into the game is very often an instinctive love of politics. It is born in many men. It is in their blood. It is, after all, the great American game, and more people are actively interested in it than baseball, football, horse racing, or poker. And they are getting more numerous all the time . . . . [the professional politician] makes enemies as well as friends. He has to turn people down. He disappoints others about jobs. He loses his temper with others, but he makes more friends than he does enemies, and the more friends he makes the surer his foothold in politics.[1]

One of Kent's co-workers on the Baltimore *Sun* shared his view of politics as a "great game," but a game which could be witnessed only with total skepticism, utmost cynicism, and absolute incredulousness.

> I enjoy democracy immensely. It is incomparably idiotic, and hence incomparably amusing . . . . In the long run it may turn out that rascality is an eradicable necessity to human government, and even to civilization itself—that civilization at bottom is nothing but a colossal swindle. I do not know. I report only that when the suckers are running well the spectacle is infinitely exhilarating. But I am, it may be, a somewhat malicious man: my sympathies, when it comes to suckers, tend to be coy. What I can't make out is . . . how can any man be a democrat who is sincerely a democrat? [2]

The authors of a basic public administration textbook observed in their latest edition that "politics, which some blasé intellectuals regarded as merely a game, is now recognized as a serious business." [3] But Harold Stein, author of the classic "Stein casebook" in public administration, is forced to observe that

> The individual administrator can do very little about changing the rules of the game; his task is to carry out his job under the rules as they exist, and the rules require him to deal with the forces that seek to deal with him. [4]

And, finally, as recently as 1968, Cesar Chavez went to Washington, D.C. in an effort to determine the nature of the rules of the game, and how they were applied—"All we want from the government is the machinery, some rules of the game."

But if Chavez was unfamiliar with these rules, it is equally apparent that the "game theory of politics"—used here in the non-mathematical sense—has a venerable lineage in the literature of American politics. How the game is supposed to be played needs to be understood if one is to have an understanding how the administrative system fits into the overall pluralist-bargaining-incremental process.

### The Containment of Conflict

When limited resources are distributed in the form of marginal increments to as wide a range of groups as possible, the very delicate allocative balance that results can be upset quite easily. That is, if a group tries to get material gains that substantially exceed the incremental allocation it can normally expect to receive, those extra gains can be obtained only at the expense of some other group(s). Under these circumstances, the group(s) deprived can be expected quite naturally to resist the efforts of the acquisitive group as strenuously as they can. In another context this has been referred to by John Kenneth Galbraith as the force of countervailing powers [5] which, in itself, is vaguely similar to Newton's third law of motion—that is, for every action there will be an equal and opposite reaction.

A basic tenet of the group theory of politics is, of course, that every participant can be expected to maximize his own self-interests. Although the notion of self-interest is embedded in the pluralist-bargaining-incremental framework of analysis, it is also common in other theories that lead far away from the pluralist-bargaining-incremental scheme. The concept of man as a rational, self-interested, satisfaction-maximizing individual is central to the views of a growing and impressive array of political scientists and political economists who have decided to designate their general intellectual focus as the "public choice" philosophy.[6] The general features of this approach are more analytical than are those of the pluralist-bargaining-incremental approach and yet more normative than the central elements of rational-comprehensive analysis to be discussed in the chapter to follow. Self-interest is also an integral feature of much of the work of scholars who may be designated as administrative humanists; their philosophy will be examined in the final chapter. For the advocates of public choice self-interest leads to rational choice; for the administrative humanists it provides the basis for organizational egalitarianism. For the incrementalist, however, it is the essence of political conflict and, as such, it is what the great game of politics is all about.

Conflict is an essential element of any game, and the ultimate object of most games is to reach a point where the conflict can be resolved—win, lose, or draw—in an orderly, nonviolent fashion. The "Great Game of Politics" is no different in this regard than any other game, except possibly for the heavy emphasis that is placed on the nonviolent aspect of the game. Within the scope of pluralist-bargaining-incremental politics, the maintenance of system equilibrium or stability represents *the* cardinal rule of the game. For the pluralist scheme to work at all, a stable sociopolitical environment *must* be maintained. Thus while political conflict over the allocation of resources may be viewed as a perfectly normal and, indeed, healthy symptom of the political system meeting the needs of social change, the conflict must not jeopardize the stability of the overall social and political system.

Above all else this means that the professional political participants involved in any conflicts must always be willing to negotiate, must always be prepared to compromise, and must always be willing to place the sanctity of the game ahead of all other values and interests. In a word, the highest of all political values for the true professional must be the maintenance of system stability.

In this situation, the administrator plays an important role. In many instances, he becomes the link between the private interest groups, the congressional committees, and top-level executive officials. Quite frequently the extent to which political conflicts are contained within the rules of the game depends on the success of the administrator in finding the common ground of agreement on which all other participants are willing to gather. It is the administrator who frequently is in the best position to exert a positive control over conflict situations, and within the pluralist framework, the manner in which conflict is ultimately controlled represents a factor that is critically related to the maintenance of system stability and order. The extent to which this ultimate goal can be realized depends upon the manner in which two interrelated conflict variables are controlled—intensity and scope.

### Reduction of Intensity

The relationship between intensity and conflict should be obvious. The willingness of an individual to alter his objectives, to reduce or compromise his demands, depends entirely upon how strongly committed he is to attaining his goals. As the intensity of one's commitment increases, the prospects of arriving at a negotiated, bargained, compromise settlement decrease dramatically. If a participant involved in a particular political conflict is *not* willing to negotiate, if he is *not* prepared to compromise, then obviously for this individual other values or interests assume greater importance than adhering to the rules of the game. Such an attitude can seriously jeopardize the stability of the social and political system. Under these circumstances, the question becomes one of how the intensity of one's commitment to the outcome of a particular conflict may be effectively controlled so as not to endanger the stability of the pluralist political framework. Two specific mechanisms are usually available to reduce the intensity of commitments.

In the first place, intensity may be directly related to the explicit or implicit normative assumptions in a particular policy objective. These normative assumptions usually reflect deep-rooted sociopolitical values. Intensity of commitment is directly related to the priority that the individual may assign to the particular sociopolitical values inherent in any policy objective. Thus the most effective way to reduce intensity of commitment is simply to avoid all discussion of the goals or ends of policy proposals since the value assumptions encompassed within the statement of goals will inevitably activate a high-intensity negative reaction from some segment of society.

The ultimate end sought by the government's poverty program is the elimination of poverty, just as the ultimate goal of the government's civil rights program is the end of racial discrimination. In both instances the justification of these programs can be questioned, and in both instances the answers can only be presented in normative terms. Racial discrimination is inherently bad or morally wrong in any society which wishes to classify itself as an advanced, civilized democracy; therefore it *ought* not be permitted to exist. Similarly, poverty in an age of abundance *ought* to be eliminated in order to end the degradation of human dignity that it causes. In foreign policy the main justification for American military and economic intervention into other nations since the end of World War II has been presented in terms of the threat of communism to U.S. security. Communism is bad and *ought* to be prevented from spreading.

If policy proposals are presented in terms of normative values, the probability of intense, emotionally charged debate over goals is increased; serious conflict will be avoided *only if* these values enjoy broad public support. In our sociopolitical system one simply cannot argue successfully against the value premise that communism must be contained, if not destroyed. Nor is it possible to argue effectively *for* the continuation of poverty. Herbert Spencer's *Social Statics* no longer enjoys reputable standing in any discussion of social welfare, although one need only go back to the end of the 19th century to note the effects of social Darwinism on the public policy process. The emotional, value-laden atmosphere that prevailed at that time in connection with the various attempts by the national and by some state governments to enact social legislation was essentially similar to the atmosphere that prevailed until quite recently (or still does prevail, some would say) in connection with the racial problem in America. In both instances substantial segments of the body politic argued openly that poverty was a natural state of affairs for some persons and that black men were inherently inferior people. Initial attempts to end poverty and racial discrimination were met with highly charged emotions from individuals both for and against the government's efforts in these areas.

In both instances the willingness to negotiate or to compromise was lost, and the stability of the political system was severely jeopardized. Since the 1930s, when social Darwinism was quietly laid to rest, the social welfare responsibility of the government has been debated in terms of specific details and operating procedures; the underlying value premise has finally become a virtually nondebatable issue. The value premises behind racial discrimination still engender intense, emotionally charged debate although it is increasingly apparent that the conflict is steadily shifting from issues of fundamental values to detailed and specific questions of practice and operations.

The pluralists hold that conflict can be controlled and system stability can be maintained as long as debate is conducted in this latter context. Discussion focused on means, not ends—on details, not goals—on specifics, not values—inevitably creates a detached, nonemotional atmosphere in which professional political participants can resolve conflict in accordance with the ultimate goal of the game—the maintenance of system stability.

The second device that the pluralists use to minimize conflict intensity is the elaborate maze of internal operating procedures that can effectively neutralize personal emotional involvement. Congress is probably the best example of just how a jungle of procedure can smother a sense of intense commitment. Newly elected Congressmen and Senators, over the years, have arrived in Washington on the crest of a "cause," fully committed to change society for the better in a small yet significant way, only to emerge years later fully committed to the sanctity of the legislative process. The complex committee-subcommittee structure, the behavioral norms of the Senate and the House, and the involved rules of parliamentary procedure that govern the floor action in both Houses are designed to insure that limited governmental resources will be allocated incrementally on the basis of bargained agreements. In this arena, the successful participant is the one who becomes an expert in the techniques of the legislative process. It is this individual who can transform the normative political values of a policy proposal into a specifically detailed legislative bill, and who can then guide the bill through the maze of the legislative process and lead it to final enactment. However, it is also this individual who can lead the bill into the legislative maze and insure that it will never be seen again.

In the administrative structure a thorough knowledge of internal operating procedures is similarly imperative. The strict rigidity and formal impersonality of the structure, like those qualities in Max Weber's classic model of bureaucracy, are usually quite sufficient to overpower intense dedication and normative commitment. Possibly the classic, tragicomical example of deliberate bureaucratic inertia has involved the military's method of "processing" requests from U.S. servicemen for permission to marry foreign nationals. Old World War II movies invariably included a standard scene of the kindly chaplain who could perceive true virtue behind the emotional intensity of the cherub-cheeked private and his foreign love. Fortunately for the young lovers, the padre's verbal endorsement was good enough for the Commanding General, who incidentally used to pitch pennies with the chaplain back in the good old days when they were boyhood friends. The red tape was cut, the couple was married in 48 hours, and the scene faded out. However, for those servicemen who were unable to unite the support of the chaplain and the General, the process was extended until, if and when approval finally was obtained, the serviceman either had been shipped out or the romance had faded—which, after all, was what the process had intended to accomplish in the first place. A more homespun tale of bureaucratic red tape is found in T. Harry Williams's prize-winning biography of Huey Long. On one occasion, the flamboyant Louisiana governor discovered that the Ringling Brothers and Barnum and Bailey Circus was scheduled to open in Baton Rouge on a night when Long's cherished LSU Tigers had a home football game. He immediately made a long-distance phone call to the circus owner, John Ringling North, whose show was then appearing in Texas. The governor's suggestion that the Baton Rouge opening be shifted to avoid the conflict was summarily rejected by North, who obviously felt that a legally binding contract made in good faith was solid enough ground to support his strong opposition to Long's proposal. As Williams describes the situation, the governor, who had dug up the provisions of an obscure 1930 animal dipping (that is, disinfecting and quarantine) law, moved gently.

> All right, Huey said amiably, but Louisiana had a dip law, and as he interpreted the act, animals crossing the state line would have to be dipped and then placed in quarantine for three weeks. "Did you ever dip a tiger?" he inquired pleasantly. "Or how about an elephant?" Mr. North said the circus would go to New Orleans that Saturday night.[7]

By keeping political conflicts focused on the discussion of means and not ends, and by maintaining an involved, complicated internal set of operating procedures, the bargaining-incremental process can unfold in a well-contained and highly predictable manner which is specifically designed to minimize conflict intensity. The bargaining-incremental process, to work best, must be conducted exclusively by professional political actors who have been completely desensitized to the emotional elements of normative values. By definition the professional within the pluralist framework is one who willingly accepts the rules of the game and who studiously masters the operating techniques that control the game. For these individuals there is no fear of becoming engulfed in the intensity of policy goals. The means become the ends, and the way the game is played becomes more important than the substance of the final output. Standing on common ground with other professionals, the negotiator is fully prepared to enter into conflict situations with a relatively accurate estimation of how all other participants in the conflict will behave. They, too, will adhere to the rules of the game because they are professionals for whom the respect of their peers is the highest reward that they can hope to attain. Guided by the axiom that applies to the true professional of any game—humble in victory, stoic in defeat—the professional political participant is intensely and emotionally committed only to the preservation of system stability and the sanctity of the pluralist-bargaining-incremental process.

### Limitation of Scope

The second variable that must be controlled if system stability is to be maintained is the scope of conflict. The prime tactics of the game—negotiation, bargaining, compromise—can be effectively applied by the professionals only if conflict can be isolated, fragmented, and limited to an essentially subnational scope.[8] If, however, the scope of the conflict cannot be effectively contained, two consequences generally result, both of which can seriously jeopardize the stability necessary for the bargaining-incremental process to function effectively. In the first place, the number of individuals interested in and/or affected by the outcome of the conflict obviously increases as the scope of conflict expands. That is, increased scope yields increased participation. Inevitably this means that more individuals who are untrained in either the rhetoric or the values of the pluralist political process will become involved in the conflict. The zone of viable negotiation, which can be controlled almost exclusively by the professionals as long as conflict can be narrowly contained, diminishes substantially when the bargaining arena is forced to absorb a high influx of amateur advocates.

When the nonprofessional enters into a conflict situation he introduces many of the elements that the professional is committed to ignore—idealistic naïveté, strong normative orientations, and emotional intensity. As a consequence, system instability dramatically increases while the prospects of a compromise solution arrived at by professionals within a collegial atmosphere visibly evaporate.

An expanded scope of conflict yields a second consequence which is very closely related to the first. The pluralist political process is adequately structured and equipped to handle a housewife's protest against consumer prices that occurs in Rome, New York. It is even equipped to handle identical but uncoordinated protests that may erupt in Rome, Georgia; Rome, Ohio; and Rome, Tennessee. If, however, the protest expands and becomes a coordinated effort including all housewives from Rome, Maine to Rome, Mississippi and from Rome, Pennsylvania to Rome, Oregon, then the pluralist political framework seriously malfunctions. The problems associated with racial discrimination in America prior to the 1960s were viewed primarily in subnational terms by the system's professional players. Not until the 1960s did the American black movement develop a high degree of national visibility. At the present time, the impact of the problem has become truly national, and commitments to the outcome of events are especially intense. Given this situation the logical question would seem to be to what extent the pluralist political system can respond effectively to the needs and wants not only of the black community in America but also of any other group or movement capable of generating a momentum that would transcend the limited, subnational scope of the pluralist system itself. It is a question which will serve as the central focus for the remainder of this book.

The very essence of the strategic game of politics is the heavy emphasis placed on the setting of limits. The limited conflict that unfolds in allocating limited resources to attain limited goals forms the basis of the pluralist-bargaining-incremental process. As a result of the strong commitment to the incremental allocation of limited resources, the professional players in the process define reality in terms of their own limited sphere of interests. Conversely, any effort to obtain a comprehensive view of the public policy process is considered futile as well as unnecessary. It is futile because, given the intellectual limitations of man, it results only in a distorted and unreal view. It is unnecessary because, if change is restricted to incremental (that is, small and extremely limited) alterations of existing programs, no great damage can ever result to the system. Therefore, although formal, overall coordination is neither necessary nor desirable, the overlapping checks and balances of the system operate in such a manner that an unwise move by any single unit within the system will inevitably be spotted and corrected by the countervailing actions of other units within the system.

### The Value Base of Pluralism

Viewed from one perspective, incrementalism may be seen solely as an administrative technique or device that can be employed to improve the operating efficiency of the executive structure. For the administrator, it provides an effective method of allocating limited resources, maximizing the stability of the pluralist political system, and controlling conflict. In other words, the incremental approach can be viewed as any other management device that is used as an allocative and conflict control mechanism.

But the strategic game of politics is not a game of chess involving the manipulation of inanimate objects. It involves the manipulation of human attitudes, values, and beliefs which frequently manifest themselves in intensely conflicting interactions. It involves a strategy always aimed at the search for the ultimate pluralist goals of stability, consensus, agreement. Therefore, the incremental scheme, presented as purely an objectively and dispassionately applied administrative device, provides only a surface view of the strategy. Incrementalism, as seen within the pluralist framework, is much more than this. It represents a state of mind, a frame of reference, a total view of human behavior. As such, it is steeped deeply in value judgments, and the value biases which rest at the base of the strategy must be revealed and analyzed.

For example, as has been indicated previously, a central feature of the incremental strategy is that the participants must be professionals who are thoroughly familiar with the rules of the game, and who are totally committed to the Grantland Rice dictum: It isn't whether you win or lose that counts, it's how you play the game. To attain the goals of consensus, stability, and agreement, amateur gamesters must be screened out; but, given the essentials of democratic theory, an elitist tone may be detected in this position as suggested previously in reference to Walker's critique of incrementalism.[9] To overcome this objection, the political pluralists have devised a rationale that places the professional political participant squarely in accord with the age-old traditions of democratic theory. What may be referred to as the marginal utility model of political participation has been expertly devised by the leading pluralist theorists. For comparative purposes, this model stands in contrast to the pure "responsible citizen" model of political participation. A brief description of the two should place the former in its proper perspective.

The responsible citizen model is based on a set of rather simplistic notions concerning human motivations, behavior, and political participation. It assumes that the average citizen is a rational individual who will, in fact, *want* to participate in politics out of a sense of civic duty, pride, and obligation. The rewards thus gained through participation may be either material or symbolic, but an intrinsic reward that is always present is the symbolic satisfaction gained through participation *per se*. The loop is thus closed between citizen participation and symbolic or material rewards or both; participation yields rewards, which in turn yield greater participation. The only difficulty with this model is that it simply does not provide an accurate reflection of objective reality when applied to a nation-state of over 200 million persons. The experience that does support the responsible citizen model has been drawn from samples involving far fewer participants—the Greek city states, the Swiss cantons, the New England town meetings. For a modern nation-state involving millions of participants, however, it seems totally inapplicable. In the United States alone, for example, the sense of duty or civic pride seems to have had little effect on the level of political participation among the body politic, especially when viewed in terms of the most basic form of personal political expression, the vote. The steady increase in the scope and intensity of political participation that has characterized the 1960s will be discussed in a later chapter. The main point to be stressed here is that while advocates of the responsible citizen model were distressed and dismayed by the seeming lack of interest being paid to the concept of civic responsibility during the late '40s and throughout the '50s, pluralist theorists utilized this phenomenon to form the basis of a theoretical model which could justify the concept of limited participation within the context of traditional democratic theory.

The marginal utility model of political participation focuses on individual motivations and behavior with a much greater degree of psychological sophistication than its responsible citizen counterpart. For the pluralist, an individual becomes involved in the political process in order to fulfill a *tangible* need. Needs create anxiety, and one way to reduce individual anxiety is through participation in the political process. The incremental strategy as an allocative device is thus geared to reducing anxieties of those individuals or groups who are concerned enough to become politically involved. The basic assumption of this model is that individuals with needs will participate to obtain tangible rewards. When these needs are even partially satisfied, individual anxiety will diminish, and continued participation in the political process becomes unnecessary. These persons then return to the status of the noninvolved, which includes for the most part, the vast majority of American citizens. Thus as long as individual needs are low, individual anxiety will also be low, and political participation will be minimized. Under these circumstances, the day-to-day operations of the political process can be effectively monopolized by the professional players.

Therefore, within the pluralist framework, one of the primary tasks of the professional political actor is to minimize the involvement of the amateur in the bargaining-incremental arena, and this is best accomplished through the alert and prudent utilization of the incremental allocative strategy. Through the partial satisfaction of needs, potentially disruptive conflict can be dissipated in its very early stages. Conflict can be limited, fragmented, contained; participation can be minimized.

The justification for this position is supported by another basic value assumption. Specifically, there is the assumption that participation indicates the evidence of needs to be satisfied; and *conversely*, nonparticipation, or noninvolvement, is sufficient evidence of the absence of needs and the presence of low anxiety and high satisfaction. For the advocate of the responsible citizen model, noninvolvement is symptomatic of a politically unhealthy society since a true sense of self-fulfillment can only be realized through active participation in the political process. For the advocate of the marginal utility model, however, just the opposite conclusion is reached: noninvolvement is symptomatic of a healthy body politic, one that is stable, satisfied, and of low anxiety. Indeed, increased involvement in the political process by the body politic is symptomatic of dissatisfaction and high anxiety which, if not checked by the incremental allocative strategies, will yield a high degree of sociopolitical instability.

### A Political Fantasy

In short, the entire pluralist theoretical network is held together by three basic value premises. First, there is the explicit assumption that participation for real, tangible, and material needs is a perfectly legitimate and highly worthy undertaking. Yet there is a very strong (albeit only implicit) bias against participation for intangible and symbolic rewards—participation by the amateur simply in search of symbolic rewards does not rank high on the value scheme of the pluralists, and they view with alarm any resurgence of participation among a wide segment of the body politic in search of intangible and symbolic rewards. Second, while participation for tangible and material rewards is a legitimate and worthy role of any citizen, his participation must take place within the pluralist political framework, and he must permit his needs to be evaluated within the context of the incremental allocative strategy. In other words, the individual must be prepared to be governed by the incremental rules of the game—which means that, at the very best, he can expect only partial satisfaction. Obviously, any individual or group refusing to accept the system's incremental allocative decisions as final or binding, or refusing to adhere to the rules of the game, is also cause for serious alarm among the pluralists. Finally, there is the basic value assumption that those who have legitimate needs to be filled will participate in the political process, and those who do not participate are satisfied and have no need for additional resources. Thus the professional political actors are relieved of any generalized sense of obligation to the body politic and are freed to concentrate their attention on the specific expressions of needs as presented by organized interest groups.

The potential consequences of this third value assumption are probably the most ominous of all. For example, the marginal utility model of the pluralists yields three possible alternative situations. First, an individual, having received partial satisfaction to his expressed need, may be prepared to disengage rationally from the pluralist political arena and voluntarily return to the status of the noninvolved. Second, the rewards gained by the individual through active participation may not be viewed as sufficient, or may even be viewed as totally insufficient to meet his perceived needs. For this individual, a general disenchantment of the political system may result, followed by a disengagement from political participation and an involuntary shift to the noninvolved category. The difference between the first and second instances is that while the first individual may disengage from the political system with a sense of partial satisfaction and a willingness to reengage again at some future date when another need may arise, the second individual may disengage with a sense of dissatisfaction which may contribute to a growing feeling of alienation, detachment, and political anomie. In this latter instance, this individual may become a permanently noninvolved, alienated, and politically detached citizen. For example, in 1937 a Roper national survey sample indicated that 35 percent of the nation's blacks felt they could not "rise in the world." In 1963, Gallup found 22 percent whites and 42 percent nonwhites in the nation were dissatisfied with their prospects for the future. To standard alienation questions, 31 percent of the nation, and 56 percent of the blacks agreed with a 1964 National Opinion Research Center survey statement that most people in the government are not really interested in the problems of the average man. In a 1966 Harris survey, 32 percent blacks and 50 percent low-income whites across the country agreed that "People running the country don't really care what happens to people like me." By 1968 the positive response by blacks to the same statement on a follow-up Harris poll had increased to 52 percent.[10]

The third possibility follows closely the pattern of the second up to the point where disengagement for the second may create a follow-up feeling of political anomie. In the third situation, disengagement may create intense anxiety, a high degree of frustration, and a high degree of aggression. The continued course of this behavioral pattern could lead not to permanent noninvolvement, but rather to the opposite—permanent and intense involvement which, if maintained, could create a high degree of political instability, social disintegration, and environmental turbulence.

The incremental system can deal with the first and second instances with relative ease, but it reveals its fundamental weaknesses when confronted with the third situation. An emotionally charged, high-intensity environment, built on resentment, frustration, and anger, is generally not conducive to the formulation of compromise proposals for conflict resolution. For administrators, especially, increased turbulence and instability create a situation in which the standard incremental strategies of resource allocation prove to be wholly inappropriate. Furthermore, the steadily increasing level and scope of individual anxiety, frustration, and aggression have seriously undermined the efficacy of the pluralists' three basic value assumptions.

First, the exclusive attention given to, and the high value placed on, the incremental allocation of material and tangible resources by the pluralists have effectively disenfranchised a growing segment of the body politic for whom intangible and symbolic rewards represent a major personal consideration. For many, the lack of a deep sense of regard for the dignity of the individual, the absence of a strong commitment to the dynamics of sociopolitical change, and the dominance of pragmatic political considerations— all characteristic of the pluralist political system—cannot be corrected simply through the exclusive manipulation of tangible and material outputs. To ignore or discount the current resurgence of normative values aimed at achieving greater intangible and symbolic rewards—for example, more responsive, effective, and equitable administrative structures—is to misread seriously the major thrust of the present force of public protest.

Second, it is now woefully apparent that the level of formal participation in the pluralist political process provides nothing in the way of an accurate indicator of the sociopolitical needs and wants that are evidenced in various sectors of the body politic. For far too many years, the pluralist system has been successful in dissecting demands for change into minute, incremental outputs that have borne little resemblance to the initially expressed need or request. As a consequence, the ranks of the disorganized, frustrated, alienated segments of society—the effectively disenfranchised—have grown steadily. Not until recently, as a result of widespread public protests, have the intangible and symbolic needs of this seemingly passive and purportedly "satisfied" group manifested themselves plainly. To continue to perpetrate the myth of the "silent satisfied majority" in majestically virtuous terms is, in itself, an exercise in utter futility.

And, finally, without intending to belabor the obvious, it should be noted that for an ever-growing segment of the "effectively disenfranchised," the rules of the pluralist game of politics have become discounted. That is, the pluralist-bargaining-incremental strategy has become meaningless, the sanctity of system stability has become incomprehensible, and the administrative structure itself has become an irrelevancy. Under these circumstances, the value base of the pluralist-bargaining-incremental process has become seriously undermined. To assume otherwise is a myopic invitation to be governed by the "hollow men" who, it will be recalled, were "distracted from distraction by distraction."

For some, the doors never close in toyland; the thrill of the great game of politics comes in trying to bring together for a fleeting moment an "unholy" coalition, a majority of minorities, that is capable of formulating a limited segment of the never-ending public policy process. How the coalition's actions contribute to some overall goal or to some overriding sense of purpose is really incidental to the strategy of the game. For the professional political actors, the play *is* the thing, and all the world *is* their stage.

For others, however, the great game reaps grim results. For a man who needs a loaf of bread for his family there are times when a half loaf simply will not do. Furthermore, the firm pluralist conviction that the future is determined by the present which is controlled by the past allows little room for innovative, imaginative concepts of change. Finally, the subnational orientation characteristic of the pluralist political system can no longer ignore, and yet is unable to cope with, the growing nationalization of political conflict in the United States. National problems require national solutions, and furthermore they require a political system in which available resources are allocated on the basis of rational and comprehensive planning. But, quite obviously, this approach can only be realized if the administrative resources of the executive branch are organized and utilized with maximum effectiveness. As seen by many observers, the federal government can achieve this end *only* if it substitutes a strategy of analysis for the more traditional strategy of games.

## Chapter IV

# THE STRATEGY OF ANALYSIS

Simply stated, the rational-comprehensive approach—that is systematic analysis—can be viewed as a clear alternative to the pluralist-bargaining-incremental model. Both approaches are concerned with making "correct" allocative decisions, but for each, "correct" decisions are formulated in entirely different contexts. The decentralized, fragmented, and subnational orientation of the incrementalist creates a public policy frame of reference entirely different from that of the rationalist whose orientation necessitates a comprehensive, system-wide evaluation of the impact of a given course of action regardless of the level or scope of the system involved. In other words, for the incrementalist a subnational orientation may be considered an essential and exclusive prerequisite, while for the rationalist the essential and exclusive prerequisite may be seen as the comprehensive, system-wide analysis of action at either the subnational, national, or transnational levels. Furthermore, the incrementalist is firmly committed to the premise that no administrative response shall be expressed in the absence of a clearly defined, tangible, material need. On the other hand, the rationalist assumes that sociopolitical needs (symbolic as well as material) must be anticipated as far in advance as possible to avoid the crisis situations which inevitably result when possible future developments are ignored until they manifest themselves in the form of angry and dynamic forces of change. In all probability, it is this latter point—the attempt to reduce future uncertainty—that distinguishes the strategy of analysis most clearly from the strategy of games.

Systems analysis is a process which is designed to relate specific operating programs to well-defined, long-range planning forecasts. It is intended, by anticipating future developments, to obtain the maximum utilization of available resources in order to influence those developments. As such, it reflects the basic paradoxical assumptions that the future is probably no less reliable a "predicter" of behavior than the past, and that, if studied thoroughly by experienced analysts, projected forecasts can provide clues valuable for anticipating future needs.

Rational-comprehensive analysis, as applied to the federal executive branch, has taken the form of a system referred to as planning-programming-budgeting, or PPB. During the Second World War management techniques such as statistical control and operations research were developed and extensively applied. After the war, these same techniques were introducd into the private business sector. For example, Robert McNamara and a group of other individuals who had worked together as a team during the war years joined the Ford Motor Company. This group, generally referred to in the industry as Ford's "whiz kids," promptly applied the advanced management techniques of systems analysis, statistical and quality control, and operations research. The Ford Motor Company was turned back from the brink of bankruptcy in large measure as a result of this group's efforts.[1]

When McNamara joined the Kennedy Administration in 1961 his management science philosophy was immediately introduced throughout the Defense Department. By 1965 McNamara had convinced President Johnson that the techniques of systems analysis could be profitably applied throughout the entire executive structure. An executive order was issued by the President in August 1965 directing all units within the federal executive branch to adopt the new planning and budgeting system (PPB).

The planning-programming-budgeting system combines the two elements of program budgeting and systems analysis. Program budgeting involves the long-range budgetary allocations of the federal government specifically to programs that are goal oriented and classified by their outputs. Systems analysis applies explicit quantitative analysis in an effort to obtain the most favorable ratio between the value of the benefits derived from any given program and the value of the resources that must be expended to obtain such benefits.

To complement the long-range planning aspect of systems analysis, the strategy of the rational-comprehensive approach requires the formulation of alternative operating programs that could be implemented to meet projected needs. The role of alternatives in the rational-comprehensive approach, an essential element of the strategy of analysis, will be discussed in more detail below. Given the policy goals to be attained, top-level executive officials must be able to rely on administrative subordinates to develop a series of meaningful and relevant alternative programs that could be implemented to attain these goals. For example, if a general policy goal of the Department of Health, Education, and Welfare is to raise the level of physical well-being of the body politic over the next 15 to 20 years, how may its resources for preventive medicine be best utilized to contribute to this goal? One study by HEW officials attempted to measure the impact of various alternative programs by analysis of comparable data. Measurable components analyzed included program costs, savings due to programs, benefit-cost ratio, number of deaths averted, and program cost per death averted. On the basis of these results, HEW analysts were able to group and rank-order the alternative programs on the basis of the most favorable benefit-cost ratios. The resulting rank-order was:

1st: Motor vehicle accident and injury prevention programs
2nd: Arthritis
3rd: Uterine cervix cancer control
4th: Lung and breast cancer prevention
5th: Syphilis control
6th: Tuberculosis control

On the basis of the overall study, HEW analysts concluded that "an investment of twenty percent additional funds for the 1968–1972 period would support these programs which show very favorable benefit-cost ratios, and which have good prospects for significant reductions in annual deaths and morbidity from selected diseases." [2] Similarly, Defense Department officials during the period when Robert McNamara served as Secretary of Defense were constantly called upon to devise program alternatives that accounted for a wide range of future contingencies. One practice that was established to deal as realistically as possible with future uncertainties was the preparation of "BOP" estimates. Through the manipulation of selected variables by program analysts, the Secretary was able to obtain estimates of the consequences of each alternative proposal under three different sets of possible future conditions—best, optimistic, and pessimistic (BOP).

Because systems analysts emphasize the formulation of alternatives, it is essential that these program proposals include meaningful and relevant alternatives. For example, at least one high-ranking official within the Nixon Administration, Henry Kissinger, feels that the BOP estimates have become administrative fetishes that provide scant guidance for top-level executive decision-makers.

> Ask the bureaucracy to examine a problem and reach the most rational solution for the nation, Kissinger has found, and what comes back is a series of arguments designed to protect the positions of individual organizations within the bureaucracy.

> Kissinger has been telling associates that the bureaucracy performs so predictably bad that, asking for optional solutions to any problem, he can always count on each part of the bureaucracy sending him three choices—not two, not four, not five, but three. And they will be worded so that any reasonable man will pick number two.[3]

When a set of alternative proposals is reviewed and a decision is finally made to implement one of the suggested programs, a third phase of systems analysis—program evaluation—goes into effect. Program evaluation is a necessary element of the rational-comprehensive approach, and its application must be continuous if its benefits are to be realized. For instance, a ten-year projected estimate of the medical needs of the nation may suggest that by the end of that period, fifty new, major medical centers will be needed throughout the nation. Assume that top-level executive officials accept the study as a reliable forecast, and a particular program proposal is selected to implement the study's recommendations. After two years of implementation, the original ten-year plan has become an eight-year projection, and as a result of constant program evaluation, early indications appear to suggest that other health programs instituted several years previously will yield benefits far in excess of what was originally expected. Program evaluators on the major medical centers project recognize this development as being directly related to their own project, and immediately start to devise a series of alternative stand-by programs which could be applied if the related developments stemming from the other health programs are subsequently confirmed. Two more years elapse and the benefits to be gained from the other health programs can now be clearly confirmed. The original estimated need for fifty medical centers may now be revised downward and the program evaluators can immediately submit their stand-by alternatives which were designed in anticipation of this new development. Whichever stand-by alternative is selected, it becomes the new program and the rational-comprehensive dialetic begins to unfold all over again— *program* leads to *evaluation* leads to *revision* leads to *new program*.

A fundamental difference between the incremental and rational-comprehensive approaches is revealed quite clearly with the latter's concern for the future and the manner in which its efforts are geared to the formulation of program alternatives that can be implemented to meet projected needs. Other substantial differences between the two approaches become apparent, however, when each is considered within its respective operational and structural framework. The most distinctive of these contrasts emerges in connection with the approach each takes toward the use of alternatives, budgetary procedures, input-output factors, centralization-decentralization patterns, and the role of politics in administration.

### Toward A More Rational Choice

Actually, the incrementalists do not rule out the role of alternatives—alternatives are, in fact, the central elements in the strategy of games. As viewed within the pluralist framework, alternatives are the wide range of preferences that emerge in the initial stages of a public policy conflict. The primary function of the incremental framework, however, is to blend these conflicting preferences, or alternatives, into a consensual composite. The search for agreement is preceded by a bargaining-negotiating-compromising process whereby all alternatives are reshaped into a composite policy. To recall Paul Diesing's description of political decision-making,

> The best available proposal should never be accepted just because it is the best; it should be deferred, objected to, discussed, until major opposition disappears. Compromise is always a rational procedure even when the compromise is between a good and bad proposal.[4]

For the rationalists, on the other hand, alternatives are handled quite differently. In the first place, a deliberate effort is made to generate as wide a range of alternative programs as possible. In the second place, at least in the early stages of analysis, each alternative stands or falls on its own merits. This is to say that once a series of program alternatives has been formulated, each is then examined in terms of cost-benefit analysis. (In the literature, cost-benefit analysis is also referred to as cost-effectiveness, or cost-efficiency analysis; [5] the terms are synonymous.) The analysis itself is aimed at estimating the total costs of each alternative as well as the total benefits to be derived from each. A cost-benefit ratio can then be calculated for each program alternative, and, theoretically at any rate, that alternative which has the highest ratio of benefits over costs should be selected. More will be said about this point later on in this chapter.

The criticism aimed at the rationalist-comprehensive approach falls most heavily on the cost-benefit aspect. The basic question raised by critics is whether public policy should be determined, shaped, or influenced on the basis of comparative cost ratios. To accept the strategy of cost-benefit analysis as a valuable and essential aid in the allocative decision-making process depends on the extent to which one is persuaded that the ratios that ultimately prevail are accurate and reliable measures of both costs and benefits.

For example, consider an issue that was settled long ago: Should first-class mail be cancelled by hand or by machine? Between these two alternatives a relatively simple cost-benefit analysis could be conducted. The salaries of the necessary number of men needed to cancel the mail by hand could be compared to the initial purchase cost of the machine, its projected maintenance costs, and the salaries of the men needed to run the machine. The next step would be to calculate the benefits derived from each alternative, and in this case the only objective benefit to be gained could be defined as the number of letters cancelled per hour. Once this benefit was calculated for each alternative, then comparative cost-benefit ratios could be determined. In this instance the significance of the analysis is obvious because only tangible, objectively defined variables were considered. For the section supervisor who directed three teams of ten men each in cancelling mail by hand, however, the prospects of supervising instead three machines with two operators each may not have been viewed casually. A supervisor of thirty men reduced to the supervision of six men and three machines may quite naturally be expected to become anxious over the security of his own position. But even if his own position is in no way jeopardized, the drastic reduction of his domain—his power, his sphere of influence—may very well create severe psychic distress by his fear of loss of status, reputation, or prestige or all of these. His morale may diminish, adversely affecting his own job performance. Thus, what was previously viewed as a benefit for the organization has been converted into a cost factor that could significantly affect the final, overall cost-benefit ratio. To make accurate and rational decisions as opposed to intuitive guesses, the systems analyst must be prepared to take into account intangible as well as tangible factors in the calculation of cost-benefit ratios. This means, of course, that intangible costs and benefits must somehow be converted into tangible, dollar amounts, or into whatever quantitative measurement is used to calculate comparative cost-benefit ratios.

The critics of cost-benefit analysis assume that intangible factors, and especially value preferences, simply cannot be converted into quantitative terms. One man's pleasure may be another man's pain, but the vast majority of individuals will assume various, fluctuating positions in between the two extremes. According to the incrementalists, an attempt to measure the unmeasurable benefits is a futile exercise. Moreover, the calculation of costs is not without its deficiencies as well. The most aggressive and articulate critic of cost-benefit analysis, as it has been applied in political decision-making, has been Aaron Wildavsky. Wildavsky notes that in choosing one alternative program over another the decision-maker—unless embarked on a mission of political suicide—must somehow take into account the political, prestige, reputational, status, and power costs (and presumably benefits as well) that are involved in each alternative.[6]

For the most part, the analysts themselves have been the first to admit their own limitations in this regard. Quite clearly there are many important—even critical—determinants that cost-benefit analysis may never be capable of calculating. The rationalist, however, is convinced that a partial analysis is better than no analysis at all, and that while intuition may still have to be employed extensively in the strategy of analysis, these intuitive "guesses" will be made explicit and subject to intensive evaluation. It is probably this latter point which represents, for the rationalist, the major advantage to be gained from cost-benefit analysis.

The use of cost-benefit techniques as an essential element of Defense Department systems analysis has been extensively evaluated.[7] The attempted application of cost-benefit analysis in other executive departments whose programs are more exclusively—or elusively—oriented toward sociopolitical goals is viewed as a failure by some [8] and as discouraging by others.[9] Nevertheless, Frederick Mosher documents in superb detail a major effort that was exerted to introduce rational-comprehensive planning and cost-benefit analysis into the State Department during the Kennedy-Johnson years.[10] As Mosher indicates, one of the many factors that worked against the State Department systems approach from the outset was, ". . . the complexity and intangibility of much of modern foreign policy and operations in contrast to the hardware and logistical base of the Pentagon." [11] Because of this factor, State Department analysts were forced to rely on intuition and subjective judgments to an even greater extent than their Defense Department colleagues.

The main thrust of this aspect of the strategy of analysis is away from the consolidation of conflicting preferences in the form of a composite, patchwork solution. It moves, instead, in the opposite direction toward a clear and precise demarcation of possible alternatives. The efforts of the incrementalist are directed toward covering up differences and camouflaging dissent; disagreement is eliminated or minimized through the gross exploitation of agreement. The rationalist assumes the position that agreement can only be reached through the full and open comparative analysis of differences, and, hence, every effort must be made to insure that the basic values, hidden biases, as well as objective facts of each alternative proposal are stated as precisely and as explicitly as possible. In this regard, alone, the difference between the two approaches is quite dramatic.

## The Cross-Strategies of Budgets and Appropriations

A second substantial difference emerges between the two approaches in the manner in which budgetary procedures are employed. Within the pluralist political system, the annual appropriations process staged in Congress is simply part of the great game, and in this context especially the incremental administrator is expected to adhere faithfully to the basic rules of the game. Every major executive unit appears before the House and Senate Appropriations Committees once a year to explain how its funds, received from Congress the previous year, have been expended, and to justify requests for funds for the forthcoming year. The rules and the strategies of this aspect of the game are intricate and subtle,[12] but two major features of the budgetary process need to be stressed here. First, funds are appropriated for only one fiscal year. At the end of the fiscal year (June 30) any unobligated funds must be returned to the U.S. Treasury. Near the end of the fiscal year the administrator must return to Congress for its review and approval of his proposed budget for the following fiscal year. Thus the annual budget and review sessions constitute something like a budgetary treadmill in constant motion on which administrators and legislators must run continuously simply to inch ahead incrementally.

The second major feature of the budgetary game is the concept of base budgeting. Assume a small executive agency operates on an annual budget of $500,000, of which $75,000 is allocated for staff and clerical salaries. Once the appropriations committees have approved the $75,000 figure it becomes part of the base operating expense ($500,000), and as long as the salary item remains constant (excluding normal cost-of-living increases), the congressional committees normally will not reevaluate this item in the future annual review sessions. A decision is made to add an associate director at $15,000 per year. The new budget proposal would then reflect the $75,000 in salaries that constituted the base, plus a request for $15,000 in new funds. The congressional appropriations committees would focus on the new request and require a full justification for the additional funds. If approved by Congress, the base figure for the agency's salary line would advance from $75,000 to $90,000, and in subsequent years the appropriations committees would accept this figure without close inspection as long as it remained constant.

What this means in practical terms to the executive-branch administrator is that—in classic incremental language—the future is defined by the present which is controlled by the past. In terms of planning it means that the future extends the length of one fiscal year and that day-to-day operations become the all-consuming preoccupation of the administrative staff. Under these circumstances, the "good" administrator is one who can ingeniously devise quick, "band-aid" solutions to conflict situations that erupt within his jurisdiction. The conciliator, the broker, the manipulator, these are the character types Congress looks for in an administrator, and the individual who has such a temperament can have substantial effectiveness with Congress. For the administrator of a different type, the one who utilizes his agency's resources to scan the sociopolitical horizon in anticipation of future needs, comparable rewards are not forthcoming from Congress. For the rationalist-comprehensive advocates, this is precisely the direction the strategy of analysis follows in connection with the budgetary process.

For the rationalist, the one-year appropriations process represents an irrational and totally insurmountable constraint on the effective and efficient utilization of available resources. The construction of a building, or a public welfare program, or an intercontinental ballistic missile program cannot be completed in one fiscal year, and it cannot be started unless the funds necessary for its completion have been guaranteed. Thus the thrust of the rationalist is in the direction of multi-year budgeting which seeks a single appropriation covering a specified period of time—two, three, even five years. The opposition to multi-year budgeting, however, is considerable. Despite herculean efforts by former Secretary of Defense Robert McNamara to establish within the Defense Department a rationalist-comprehensive orientation, his goals were frequently thwarted by the incrementally attuned congressional appropriations process. For example, in 1963 McNamara and other top executive officials of the Kennedy Administration, in an effort to implement the first phase of a multi-year projected foreign aid program, made a concerted effort to get congressional approval for a $4.52 billion foreign aid bill. Congress finally approved $3 billion for the program on 30 December 1963, which, incidentally, was the end of the sixth month of the 1964 fiscal year. Of this amount, $1 billion was appropriated for military assistance funds although the Administration had requested $1.405 billion. In 1964 McNamara returned to Congress to make his presentation for fiscal year 1965 military assistance funds. His mood of bitterness was clearly apparent as he delivered the same statement to both the House Foreign Affairs Committee and the House Appropriations Subcommittee on Foreign Operations (the Passman Subcommittee).

> Last year when I appeared before this committee I stated that we hoped to reduce the military assistance program to about $1 billion a year by 1968. But neither I nor the Clay Committee which supported my hope . . . believe that our security could be properly protected by such a low level of appropriations in fiscal year 1964 and 1965. We are presenting a request of only $1 billion for fiscal year 1965 *solely* because the Congress has made it crystal clear to the executive branch that it is unwilling to appropriate a larger amount.[13]

It was McNamara's contention that the congressional reductions in the military assistance appropriations requests had caused serious, if not irreparable damage insofar as the operating efficiency of the Defense Department's mission was concerned. Passman's reaction was immediate.

> Passman: . . . It is not quite fair to the committee and the Congress to . . . come down and ask for $1 billion and then have the record show it is an inadequate amount.
>
> McNamara: I think it is clear.

Passman: Not as far as I am concerned.

McNamara: Let me clarify for you. The record is very clear that the executive branch for several years has requested more funds than the Congress authorized and appropriated. Specifically, last year the President requested $1.405 billion and Congress appropriated $1 billion. There can be no responsibility for the cut of $405 million other than on the shoulders of Congress.[14]

McNamara was criticized by many congressmen for what appeared to them to be an abdication of administrative responsibilities. McNamara addressed himself to this criticism. "I recognize the point of principle you make. I think it is my responsibility to tell you what I believe we need, not to judge what is in your mind or what is likely to come out of the teller box." He then added, "On the other hand, I think you must recognize your responsibilities to the executive branch to act somewhat in line with the amounts requested and to act on a timely basis." [15]

Given his perception of a strong executive and his administrative expertise, McNamara viewed his accountability to Congress solely in terms of providing general, overall policy review. Insofar as day-to-day operating decisions were concerned, McNamara felt his accountability extended directly and exclusively to the President. In other words, Congress was not qualified to oversee the administration of operating details, nor was it adequately equipped to review and evaluate operating decisions. The rationalist-comprehensive orientation which McNamara sought to establish within the Defense Department reflected his basic assumption that once Congress approved a general policy it was his responsibility to insure that the policy was implemented as efficiently and effectively as possible. In any event, the choice of the manner of implementation should be the exclusive prerogative of the chief administrative officer, accountable only to the chief executive official of the government, the President.

Obviously this attitude clashes with the basic incremental approach which focuses sharply on means, not ends; on programs, not policies; on details, not generalities. The range of issues open to bargaining is much broader when means rather than ends are the issues; and hence the incremental approach is politically much more desirable than the role afforded to legislators and their committees within the rationalist-comprehensive framework. McNamara was able to demonstrate that the strategy of analysis, when applied to the allocative process, is technically sound and administratively feasible. Unfortunately he was not able to demonstrate convincingly that his approach was politically more desirable than the incremental scheme. It is in this context that the concept of multi-year budgeting must be viewed; and it should now be apparent that, insofar as the incrementalist is concerned, the political costs of multi-year budgeting over the traditional one-year appropriation cycle substantially negate any administrative benefits that may be gained.

### How To Measure Effectiveness?

Still another substantial difference between the two approaches involves their different attitudes towards input-output questions. It has been suggested that the incremental allocative system is predominately oriented towards input, while the rationalist-comprehensive approach is predominately oriented towards output. The contrast between these two orientations in public administration may be clarified if one first considers the input-output scheme as it has developed in the private, profit-making corporation or business enterprise.

For the elder Henry Ford, in the early days of the mass produced Model As and Model Ts, inputs were represented by finished parts and material, workers, plants and factories, an astute perception of public needs, and entrepreneurial skill. Ford's attitude toward outputs was much more simplistic: "Paint them any color as long as they are black." Outputs were related to goals; the basic goal for Ford was profit; the production of automobiles was the only output that needed to be considered. What this meant in terms of private organizational analysis and evaluation was that a single factor—profit—could be used to measure the standard of overall organization performance. If profits were high and rising, then by definition the organization was utilizing its inputs most efficiently. If, however, profits were low or falling, this fact was a clear indication of either a decreasing quality of inputs, or the poor utilization of the inputs within the internal structures of the organization. The influence of such scholars as Frederick W. Taylor, Lionel Urwick, and James Mooney on business organizations was substantial and enduring. If nothing else these scholars established internal operating efficiency as a basic principle of success. An efficiently operating company would be a successful company in that its profits would increase. Low or declining profits were a positive indicator of some internal malfunction.

The effects of this corporate, profit-oriented attitude within the governmental sector of our society are considerable. Government, of course, is widely recognized as not being engaged in profit-related activities. Furthermore, most of the major outputs of government are intangible "products" which cannot be quantitatively measured. Thus with no profit motive and no tangible outputs (or relatively few and minor ones), the orientation of political and administrative officials toward governmental efficiency is directed toward inputs and toward relating inputs to internal operating procedures. The executive for Ford Motor Company can tell if he is doing a good job if his sales and profits increase. In this context, the customer has dollars to spend, and the best indicator of customer satisfaction is found in sales figures. The public administrator, however, has nothing to "sell" in a tangible or profit-related sense. Yet he, too, has customers; to the extent that he is convinced that customer satisfaction represents a reliable indicator of internal operating efficiency and managerial effectiveness, he is vitally concerned about customer satisfaction.

How can this element of customer or client satisfaction be measured within governmental circles? At this point one of the basic value assumptions of the pluralist system takes effect. Namely, the absence of a clearly articulated and formally presented expression of dissatisfaction must be interpreted as a clear indication of the effective and efficient management of internal operations which, in turn, must indicate that inputs are being utilized properly. The expression of *legitimate* dissatisfaction, on the other hand, must be indicative of internal malfunctioning which, in turn, means the improper utilization of inputs. Thus for many years the answer to the dilemma of public education in America was the construction of more schools, just as the need for low-income housing was answered by the construction of more public housing projects, and the transportation problem was attacked by building new super-highways. In short, within the pluralist context, the expressions of dissatisfaction coming from the body politic can best be met through a redoubling of efforts, that is, by increasing inputs which will inevitably increase outputs and decrease dissatisfaction. Thus conflict control becomes a function of allocative control—the manipulation of dissent is accomplished through the manipulation of tangible and material resources. The final judgment of success for the pluralist system is how well inputs are manipulated to minimize dissent and not what outputs are produced to attain some broad social goal.

The strategy of analysis, on the other hand, stresses the process of converting resources, or inputs, into programmatic outputs, or purposeful ends. Thus the rationalist's orientation towards output is directly related to the specific program alternative selected; this selection, in turn, is directly related to an overall policy goal. For example, the major goal of the Department of Transportation is to "develop national transportation policies and programs conducive to the provision of fast, safe, efficient, and convenient transportation at the lowest cost consistent therewith." A first step of the rationalist would be to convert this broad policy directive into operationally valid terms. For instance, "fast" could be defined in terms of the time required to move people or things between specified points in the United States. One function of any program alternative, therefore, would be to minimize the time necessary to move people and goods from point to point. Similarly, engineering specifications, traffic patterns, National Safety Council figures, and so forth, could provide sufficient data to establish a meaningful operational definition of "safe." In this respect, a projected schedule of preventive maintenance and functional deterioration could prove to be most meaningful. "Convenience" could be defined as another time factor (that is, less time spent waiting to move between points), or as the number of options available for moving people and goods between points. "Efficiency" could be measured as the ratio between benefits and costs. In any event, by redefining these words in operational and nonspecific terms (that is, without reference to the specific modes of transportation), it would be possible to develop a set of overall, coordinated national transportation policies; such policies could not be developed if each major subunit within the Department of Transportation were permitted to define the departmental function in its own terms.

In the pluralist-incremental context, in which inputs are decided upon to manipulate consent, operating performance can be defined according to (1) functional mode, and (2) level of demand. For the Federal Highway Administration the number of new miles of transcontinental highway opened in the preceding year may serve as a measure of output; the Federal Aviation Administration may use the number of passenger miles logged, or flight hours; and the Federal Railroad Administration may cite the number of passenger-miles-or ton-miles of freight moved as outputs. The point is that, if the Secretary of Transportation were forced to allocate his limited resources among these three major subunits, the highly specific and exclusive nature of each subunit's standard of performance would make it impossible for his decisions to be based on a comprehensive, rationally sound, comparative analysis. One cannot compare highway miles, air passengers, and tons of freight if each is viewed as the ultimate measure of output. In such a circumstance, each particular output becomes an exclusive factor, effectively isolated from any general and comparative analysis but quite responsive to political manipulation. In other words, the incremental framework virtually insures the emergence of a high-level exclusiveness which is extremely resistant to rational-comprehensive analysis. In this context, therefore, the Federal Aviation, Highway, and Railroad Administrations would emerge as the dominant agencies of the Department of Transportation, and the position of Secretary would considerably diminish in form and certainly in authority.

However, by utilizing the operationalized definitions of the Department's policy statement, an analytical approach to the allocation of limited resources could be achieved. If highway miles, air passengers, and tons of freight could be viewed as the inputs they are, and if they could be related to the nonspecific outputs of speed, safety, convenience, efficiency, and cost, then a start toward rational-comprehensive analysis could be made. For example, all three subunits could relate comparably to the goal of reducing the time needed to move people and goods between points. Choices among alternative means of high-speed intercity transportation (limited access superhighways, low-cost helicopters, or metroliner-monorail trains) could be based on their respective overall cost-benefit ratios. Applying the strategy of analysis in this manner could permit top-level officials to make comprehensive decisions concerning the choice of alternatives; but even more significantly, the use of inputs in establishing the exclusiveness of subunit performance output could be curtailed.

The effort to apply systems analysis in the State Department, though unsuccessful, was similarly designed to combine multiple subunit performance measures into a unified and meaningful standard. State Department analysts viewed the country program as the basic building block of a rational-comprehensive foreign policy. Thus within any given nation the individual program performance of various U.S. missions (for example, AID, Peace Corps, USIA) would be combined into a single country program. These programs could provide accurate evaluations of the *total* U.S. foreign affairs effort in a single nation (information that previously had never been available). Furthermore, country programs could be combined to form regional programs, thus providing top-level State Department officials with a general assessment of the world-wide balance of costs and benefits derived from the total allocation of U.S. foreign policy funds.

After an extended skirmish (1963–1967) the country program approach of the State Department was rejected in favor of the officially sanctioned PPB system which had become the primary responsibility of the Bureau of the Budget following the release of President Johnson's 1965 executive order. The PPB system reflected an agency planning orientation which required, for example, the Agency for International Development to present its information, gathered from each of its foreign missions, to the Budget Bureau in the form of a comprehensive, agency-wide program proposal. Similar requirements were made of all other foreign affairs agencies. Unfortunately, the goals of overall executive-branch program coordination sought by the Budget Bureau demolished the efforts by State Department analysts to deveop a rational-comprehensive foreign policy planning capability for use by top-level State Department officials.

## A Centralized Decision-Making Structure

The differences between the input and output orientations are in themselves quite significant; viewed in a broader context, each is directly related to the fundamental distinctions between the incrementalist and rationalist approaches. Moreover, the different outlooks on input and output highlight still another major difference between the strategies of games and of analysis, namely, the decentralization versus the centralization of executive power and authority.

From the point of view of basic pluralist theory, the rational-comprehensive approach reveals a centralizing bias which represents a major threat to the Great Game of Politics. Indeed, it is difficult to find any advocate of systems analysis who has attempted to hide the fact that the rational-comprehensive approach is designed to alter the traditionally fragmented and decentralized structures of the executive branch that control allocations. To be effectively utilized, the systems approach requires (as noted above) centralized coordination; this in turn requires a greater degree of centralized executive authority.

Some rationalist advocates have stressed the point that the strategy of analysis depends extensively on the widespread cooperation of middle- and lower-level administrative officials. William

Capron, a former Assistant Director of the Bureau of the Budget, argues that if the analytical approach is implemented correctly and effectively, the initial centralized structure will ultimately yield a highly productive decentralized decision-making apparatus.[16] But it must be noted that the type of decentralized structure Capron envisions is fundamentally different from the existing decentralized pluralist framework. As seen by Capron maximum operating authority and discretion must be delegated to subordinate administrators in order for systems analysis to operate effectively. The administrator within the analytical context, however, is constrained by explicitly stated policy goals and program objectives. Within these limits, administrative discretion may be encouraged and even rewarded, but only to the extent that the administrator's discretionary behavior is related in a direct and positive way to the attainment of specific goals and objectives. No such ultimate measure of administrative performance is applied within the incremental framework. Within the incremental context the administrator may enjoy a wide degree of discretion, but he is also relatively free from any accountability to top-level executive officials for his administrative performance. Indeed, the failure of State Department analysts to win approval for their Comprehensive Country Programming System may be viewed in terms of numerous factors, not the least of which would appear (from Mosher's account) to be the reluctance on the part of the State Department's "elite corps"—the senior Foreign Service Officers—to depart from their broadly defined discretionary behavioral base. Discretionary behavior within a context of maximum political ambiguity characterizes the essence of traditional international diplomacy. A shift to explicitly stated goals and objectives, and the application of explicit measurements of performance would have certainly strained the senior State Department Foreign Service Officers. Because the Budget Bureau's PPBS was viewed as less threatening than the State Department's own CCPS, greater support was generated from within the ranks of the senior Foreign Service Officers for the Budget Bureau's system.[17] For many administrators, the incremental framework insures the maintenance of an indispensable solitude; ironically, in this instance a rational-comprehensive system was seen as generally helping to maintain that condition.

### The End of Politics?

One final question needs to be discussed in connection with the strategy of analysis. To what extent, if any, does the rational-comprehensive model reveal a political orientation? A major criticism aimed at this approach has been that its advocates are apolitical at best, and antipolitical at worst. Moreover, there is the general impression that the decision-making nexus of the analytical model is structured exclusively within the quantitative analysis of objective and tangible economic data. Both of these points should be evaluated in some detail.

In discussing the political implications of rational analysis, Professor Aaron Wildavsky has written,

> It will be useful to distinguish between policy politics (which policy will be adopted?), partisan politics (which political party will win office?), and system politics (how will decision structures be set up?). Program budgeting is manifestly concerned with policy politics, and not much with partisan politics, although it could have important consequences for issues that divide the nation's parties. *My contention is that the thrust of program budgeting makes it an integral part of system politics.*[18]

As stated before, the public policy process is a value-laden process, but one in which the administrative structure stands as the intervening variable between values and policy outputs. As a consequence, a change in the value orientation of the political actors is no guarantee of a permanent change in the nature of public policy outputs unless there are also appropriate structural changes within the political system. The core element of every overall organization structure is its decision-making substructure. Who makes decisions is really of secondary importance to these questions: How are decisions made? What kind of decision-making structure prevails? Wildavsky is absolutely correct in contending that control of the decision-making apparatus of any organization represents the essence of system politics. To the extent that the rationalists are committed to gaining control of the executive decision-making process they are deeply and inextricably involved in a political conflict of the first magnitude.

Yet the rationalist is obviously not a political animal in the pluralist-incremental tradition. The antipolitical image of the rationalist projected by his critics may be accurate to the extent that "politics"—in the sense of the incremental allocation of limited resources on the basis of bargained agreements among professional political actors—is considered neither as efficient nor as effective as the strategy of analysis in satisfying the needs of the body politic. But to be antipolitical in this sense is not necessarily the same as being anti- or apolitical in the more inclusive sense. Rational analysis may be viewed as an administrative tool or technique, just as the incremental approach may be viewed as a tool that can be applied by administrators to solve a particular problem. There are no neutral tools in administration, however, and if, as some have contended, the analytical approach knows no politics, it will learn in short order if it is to survive. Most responsible and knowledgeable proponents of rational analysis—persons who have been most directly and officially involved in applying this approach in executive decision-making—agree that it is not a neutral, apolitical instrument. In short, there are very few individuals who would disagree with Wildavsky's central contention that political questions demand political answers. Rationalists would simply add that the search for these answers might be advanced and improved through systematic and rigorous analysis. Analytical answers or solutions, however, must be translated into a political context, and this, quite properly, is a function of the political official, not the administrative analyst. It is at this point that very strong feelings of ambiguity and distrust tend to becloud the entire rational-comprehensive approach.

## An Essential Balance

Basically, the position of the pluralists has been that the analytical approach reduces all political problems to quantitatively measurable economic terms, and in so doing it applies to the public policy decision-making process a strict gauge of economy and efficiency in lieu of a broader gauge of social equity and public welfare. Within this kind of decision-making framework, which allegedly excludes all noneconomic considerations as well as all nonquantifiable variables, the pluralists envision an impotent top-level executive echelon, including the President, whose only task will be to ratify decisions made by the new breed of apolitical, administrative mandarins.

As might be expected, the role of systematic analysis in the decision-making process, as the rationalists themselves define it, presents a drastically different picture. The analysts see themselves taking the broad policy goals presented to them by top-level political officials in the executive branch and designing a series of alternative programs to achieve the stated goals. To the maximum extent possible, quantitative data is used in preparing a cost-benefit analysis on each proposed alternative. But the analysis is by no means limited exclusively to the use of quantitative data. Intuition, common sense, logic, and educated guesses are frequently relied upon, but in each instance these techniques are clearly defined and made completely explicit. When each alternative has been thoroughly analyzed, the role of the administrative analyst technically ends and the role of the political official begins. All rationalists agree that the final selection from the proposed alternatives is basically a political decision which can only be made by political officials. Theoretically it is the political official alone who should be able to evaluate each alternative in terms of his own, intuitively devised scale of political costs and benefits. It is the President and his departmental secretaries who ultimately must apply their own set of political values to each proposed alternative, and in so doing they may very well conclude that an alternative which offers the most favorable cost-benefit ratio from the analyst's point of view would be quite costly in terms of their own political cost-benefit scale. Theoretically, then, the ultimate choice is removed from the analytical stage and placed squarely in a political context.

In actual practice, this neat demarcation between analysis and decision-making could (and probably will) become blurred. As has been previously noted, the classic distinction between administration and politics deserves a central position in our political folklore. The same objections that have again and again been raised to disprove this distinction seem applicable to the demarcation between analysis and decision-making. Furthermore, much depends on the intellectual abilities of the top-level executive officials. An effective relationship between political officials and administrative analysts will depend on the extent to which the political officials have, at least, a basic understanding of the methods of systematic analysis. Every executive official should feel free to seek advice from his staff administrators but no executive official should ever feel bound to accept their judgments. The executive official for whom rational-comprehensive analysis is totally incomprehensible may very well react defensively, negatively, even dogmatically, or he may become completely passive and pliable. In the former case, valuable benefits of analysis could be lost; in the latter, serious political costs could be ignored. One key factor, then, to systematic analysis balanced within a politically attuned framework is the calibre of men who are selected to fill the top-level executive positions, including the President. A sympathetic attitude toward the rational-comprehensive approach is not enough; an effective application of the analytical method can only be supplied by men who understand its strengths and weaknesses, its advantages and its limitations.

Taken collectively, the differences between these two methods of allocation and control are quite substantial. The rationalist's efforts to maximize his control over the future, his insistence on developing a wide range of possible alternatives to meet a given need, his reliance on cost-benefit analysis to evaluate each alternative, his efforts to attain legislative approval for multi-year funding, his output orientation, and his preference for a high degree of centralized executive authority and power, all place him at the opposite end of the spectrum from his pluralist-incremental counterpart. What emerges finally are two contrasting, composite administrative types, each reflecting different sets of facts, values, and attitudes that contribute to the overall formation of a general frame of reference for the individual administrator—a composite state of mind, so to speak. For the incrementalist, his primary frame of reference is subnational in the sense that his effectiveness is maximized if political values remain diversified, political groups retain their autonomy, political conflict is narrowly contained, and popular political activity is limited. These "goals" can best be attained within an executive structure in which administrative power and authority are extensively decentralized and available resources are allocated incrementally as a result of bargained agreements among professional political actors.

By contrast, the movement of the strategy of analysis is up, not down. The primary frame of reference for the rationalist is essentially teleological whether focused at the subnational, national, or transnational levels. Programmatic goals are established on the basis of long-range assessments of system-wide public policy priorities. The centralized mobilization of government resources to meet these goals follows as a logical consequence. One basic assumption of the rationalist is that such terms as *public interest* and *general welfare* can be made operationally valid, and that subnational, national, and transnational priorities can be established through the application of analytical methods. This assumption is based on the more fundamental one that the major sociopolitical problems confronting the nation today should be recognized as *national* problems requiring coordinated, long-range, national solutions. This essential factor in the rationalist's overall frame of reference clashes directly with the limited and fragmented subnational orientation and value system of the incrementalist.

## Chapter V

# ENVIRONMENTAL TURBULENCE

As noted throughout the previous chapters, the bargaining-incremental approach can only be applied within a sociopolitical context characterized by a low level of anxiety. As anxiety increases within the body politic, the rationale for adhering to the rules of the incremental game becomes less and less persuasive. Recently, the level of anxiety in America has increased dramatically, and in consequence the bargaining-incremental approach of the pluralists, that is, the strategy of games, has become incapable of attaining its accustomed goals of agreement, consensus, and stability. Paradoxically, the anxiety mounting throughout the nation appears to be following two divergent, though by no means exclusive, paths.

### Technical Complexity

Throughout the nation there is concern over the government's inability to provide effective solutions to an ever-increasing set of technical and logistical problems, which are broad and all-inclusive in nature. The rising number and complexity of hard-core problems that require technological and logistical solutions, when viewed from the incremental perspective of the pluralists, appear to be insoluble. For example, can the incremental approach provide effective solutions to the purely technical and logistical aspects of waste disposal in a nation of 200 million people? Does it have the capacity to develop and implement technical and logistical solutions for the growing national dilemmas of air and water pollution? Is it technically and logistically possible for the incremental approach to provide an effective set of social services for the nation's urban poor? In a supposedly golden age of abundance, can the incremental system provide effective remedies for the dismal plight of migratory farm workers? These and countless other problems clearly demand long-range planning commitments, large-scale allocative commitments, and high-level coordination, all of which run counter to the incremental approach. The plight of the innovative administrator who must work within the incremental context was described best by Norman Mailer during his 1969 mayoral campaign in New York City.

> I think it's to Lindsay's credit that he worked hard . . . to solve the problems of the city. But Lindsay has been trapped in the workings of a style of political administration which simply cannot administer the city any longer. It is impossible, in my opinion, to change this city for the better without creating a new political basis. Lindsay is the proof of this because he worked manfully in the old tradition, tried to wed a new tradition to it, and failed.[1]

On a national level the dilemma is no less acute. During the decade of the 1960s, executive-branch administrators attempted, within the incremental framework, to maintain multibillion dollar space, defense, and domestic programs but made little or no attempt to coordinate the allocation of these resources to any comprehensive set of national priorities. Political attractiveness and desirability frequently allow the thin edge of the wedge to slip innocuously into the public policy process. For example, in 1961 Congress appropriated $11 million to the Federal Aeronautics Administration to conduct a feasibility study on the development of a supersonic jet transport (SST). In view of the fact that similar planes were being advanced by the Soviet Union and a combined British-French venture, the FAA request was approved primarily on the basis of political considerations—the maintenance of the United States' prestige as a world leader in aeronautical and space technology, and the prevention of a later drain on United States' dollars. An additional $20 million was appropriated for further study in 1962.

When Pan American World Airways placed an order for six of the British-French Concordes in 1963, President John F. Kennedy announced a shift from the feasibility study stage to the full development stage of a U.S. supersonic jet. His announcement was accompanied by a request for an additional $60 million and a firm statement that, "In no event will the government investment be permitted to exceed $750 million." From 1964 to 1969 Congress appropriated a total of approximately $650 million to maintain the SST program. In 1970, President Richard M. Nixon, after conducting a review of the status of the SST, sent to Congress an appropriation request for $290 million for continued development of the plane.

Passed by the House but rejected by the Senate on 3 December 1970, the appropriations measure was sent to a House-Senate Conference Committee. Congressional approval was finally obtained to appropriate $210 million which extended the life of the program to 30 March 1971. Thus the total U.S. financial commitment to the program rose to $960 million. In March 1971 an appropriations bill to provide the Department of Transportation with funds for the final quarter of fiscal year 1971 was brought to floor votes in both the House and Senate. Contained in the bill was $134 million to extend the life of the SST to the end of the fiscal year (June 30). In a teller vote, the House deleted the SST funds from the bill, 217–179. On March 19 the Senate Appropriations Committee amended the House bill by restoring the full appropriation request for the SST, and sent the bill to the floor. Senate action came on March 24 when, by a vote of 46–51, the committee's amendment to restore the $134 million was rejected.

A final effort to revive the program was surprisingly attempted by House Republican leaders in May 1971. Opponents of the program in the House were caught unprepared, and the full House voted 201–197 to appropriate $85.3 million to restore the program. When the measure finally reached the Senate floor, the momentum of the surprise attack was lost, and on 20 May 1971 the measure was decisively defeated, 58–37.

For eleven years the SST program quietly consumed nearly one billion dollars before comprehensive analyses and discussions of the project and its relation to other issues of national public policy were conducted on a broad scale. For the three month period from January to March 1971 factual data relating predominately to the economic and environmental aspects of the program poured forth from both sides of the debate. Certainly the net effect of this extended, in-depth discussion was positive in that persuasive arguments were advanced within a relatively well-defined rational and comprehensive framework. As a result, executive-branch officials, legislators, and the body politic were finally forced to confront the SST program in terms of basic policy goals and fundamental socio-political values.

Unfortunately, even when the pluralist political system makes an effort to conduct an in-depth analysis of a particular public policy question, as it has on occasion, the net result still reflects a composite residue of the pluralist distillation process. In 1965 Congress created a special Public Land Law Review Commission to study and evaluate the Federal government's present and future policy position in connection with the 755 million acres of federally owned land. At the cost of approximately $7 million, the commission concluded its study in 1970 and presented to Congress "a perhaps predictable 342 page tapestry of compromises":

> Get rid of some of the land, but keep most of it. Give commercial interests, like the huge mining, timber, and farming industries, more leeway to make money from the public domain, but make them pay the Government more in doing so. Cut the tax-shy and land-shy states and localities in on more of the public land benefits, but reserve a goodly amount for outdoor museums and parks. . . .

> Accordingly, if the report does not emerge from the crucible of controversy as an acceptable text on land use, it will have at least earned a place in history as an example of that mysterious process known as "democracy at work." [2]

Advances in science and technology have proceeded at a pace that dramatically exceeds comparable advances in our political system. One consequence of this constantly expanding gap is the inability of government to respond to—much less to anticipate—the technical and logistical spinoffs of scientific advancement. Thus while Detroit can mass-produce cars at an astronomical rate, the public sector approaches the spinoff problems of traffic congestion and air pollution incrementally. An advanced, industrialized society creates advanced, industrialized dirt and grime which can most effectively be cleaned away with a fast acting, cold water, low-sudsing, enzyme detergent. Clothes get whiter, but rivers get dirtier while incremental environmentalists try to plan how yesterday's solutions can be applied to today's water pollution problems. Public utilities, especially electric power and telephone companies, have traditionally enjoyed a snug haven in the governmental sphere. As legalized monopolies, they have been expected to be keenly aware of public needs and wants. The success of the electric power and telephone companies has been phenomenal in one respect in this regard. All-electric homes, complete with several Princess telephones, are relatively commonplace in suburban communities. The telephone itself has become virtually a basic item in every dwelling unit, and an air conditioner is thought to be a virtual necessity for the office and the dwelling unit in nearly every major city. Increased sales of electrical appliances and telephone apparatus reflect a healthy economy, a convenient and comfortable existence. Insofar as the northeast quadrant of the nation is concerned, however, the prospects of increased summer electrical blackouts, brownouts, and telephone circuit overloads create a somewhat different picture. As consumption rates continue to spiral upward,

> This takes its toll on the environment; more hydroelectric dams, which flood surrounding lands; more steam generators, spewing fine ash and sulfur dioxide from their stacks; and more than 100 atomic-electric plants in 31 states, raising the new problem of thermal pollution in streams and the specter of accidents releasing deadly radiation.[3]

In short, the hard-core technical and logistical problems generated in an increasingly complex society seem to multiply daily, and they appear virtually immune to the efforts of well-intentioned administrators who are working within the incremental systems. The parable on democracy by Robert Michels should be recalled: two sons, following a death-bed revelation of their father, work hard and endlessly in their field to find a fictitious treasure; they never find the treasure, of course, but in the process of the search they enrich their field and develop a highly productive crop output on which they are able to maintain a comfortable existence for themselves and their families.[4] The irony is that Michels' heroes could not have been incrementalists in today's American society. For two men to work one field over a lifetime and maintain high productivity all the while would require careful planning, the systematic application of scientific methods, and an astute anticipation of future events. In a dynamically changing technological society, however, innovations tend to generate their own unique new problems. The incremental process is not designed to achieve maximum problem-solving effectiveness in the face of a rapidly expanding growth rate, be that growth rate defined in terms of population expansion, facility utilization increase, or the development of scientific knowledge. Insofar as the critical needs for basic, hard-core, technical and logistical solutions are concerned, the incremental process is inadequately designed to stem the mounting anxieties within the body politic that this situation is creating. Some form of rational-comprehensive analysis seems imperative.

## An Ethical Administrative Vacuum

If problems requiring technical and logistical solutions were the only cause, or even the major cause, of heightened public anxiety that confronts administrative officials today, one could be more confident about the future. But in addition to growing demands for effective solutions to the wide range of mounting national problems, public anxiety has been increased too by the prospect of our society becoming a computerized technocracy. This anxiety stems from personal insecurity, from fear of the loss of individual identity, a sense of political powerlessness, an increasing frustration resulting from an impersonal sociopolitical system, an inability to participate in the shaping of one's own destiny, and an unmistakable irreverence of the system for the ethical and moral integrity of the individual.

It is possible, of course, to view this anxiety as stemming from the forces of science and technology. Examples of the dehumanizing effects of advanced industrialized societies are all too familiar. From Charles Chaplin's "Modern Times," through *Brave New World, 1984,* and *The Organization Man,* man is portrayed not in the fashion of Aristotle's political animal but rather as an animal who develops a complex set of conditioned responses to the stimuli of mass, industrialized society. The politics of despair have been fashioned in the United States from the large corporate image of the private enterprise system. In the wake of the economic determinism of Karl Marx, the power elite theories of C. Wright Mills, and the warnings about the military-industrial complex from Dwight D. Eisenhower, what hope is there for man to assume an expressive, self-fulfilling role as an individual with true political value and merit? In the face of such a terrifying concentration of power in the hands of the "power elite," what alternatives does the average individual have but to accept the shape of the universe as designed by others?

This is not the place to unravel the devil theory of economic determinism; the economic motivation in man is obviously an important—in many instances, a crucial—determinant in styling his political and social behavior. An analysis of political systems and political behavior based exclusively on a theory of economic determinism, however, makes any discussion of alternative types of political systems or structures in a representative democracy totally irrelevant. If the military-industrial complex does, in fact, have the nation's means of production neatly tied up, what possible difference can any political change make, short of establishing a pure communist system? Unfortunately, for virtually the entire period marking America's industrial growth, criticism of *political-administrative* ineffectiveness and inequities has been answered in economic terms placing the critics squarely in a Marxian or un-American context. One need only recall that, as the construction workers paraded down Wall Street in fervent support of President Nixon's foreign and domestic policies, their predecessors in the American Labor Union movement were branded the worst kind of communist radicals in their efforts to gain legal sanction for the right to organize. Nor should one forget that the effort to extend the right to vote to women was viewed by many as a terrible Bolshevist plot, as was the attempt to get the federal government to pass a child labor law. The socialist-communist innuendo was effectively employed in the case of the American Medical Association's three-and-one-half-year campaign against President Truman's national health insurance program. More recently the communist conspiracy theme has been extended to include a wide range of protesting groups and individuals, regardless of the object of their criticism. Even Ralph Nader was thoroughly investigated by private detectives engaged by the General Motors Corporation. If "what's good for General Motors is good for the nation," then an enemy of that giant corporation must, by definition, be an enemy of the state. Standing in equal disdain had to be Robert Choate, the ogre of the snap-crackle-pop set, who blew the whistle on the breakfast cereal industry. For his efforts in devising the infamous Choate choke chart, he, too, was purportedly investigated by private "credit" concerns.

As a result of the efforts by the more intensely dedicated pluralists to demolish virtually every political-administrative criticism of the governmental process with an onslaught of patriotic rhetoric, many aggrieved individuals have undoubtedly felt constrained from engaging in the politics of protest and have withdrawn instead into the shell of political anomie. The net short-range result has been two-fold: first, by transposing sociopolitical criticism into an economic determinist mode, the focus of attention is shifted from specific political-administrative inefficiencies and inequities to a much broader level of conflicting political ideologies thus effectively insulating the pluralist political system from sustained criticism;

and second, by creating a potentially intimidating political atmosphere, an illusion of consensus and satisfaction has been created and maintained which, in turn, has been used to buttress the pluralist rationale.

As opposed to the relatively profitable short-term effects of the strategy of games, the long-term effects are clearly negative and potentially quite degenerative. As noted in an earlier chapter, the pluralist system recognizes that, on occasion, various groups or individuals may have to incur certain losses in the allocative process. The rules of the game provide a bromide for this contingency—humble in victory; stoic in defeat. But losses must never be allowed to become cumulative; if losses reach the point where they can never be offset by subsequent incremental gains, then the rationale for continuing to adhere to the rules of the game is destroyed. The logic of the strategy of games is sound in the abstract; in actual application, however, the pluralists are either unwilling or unable to extend the same consideration to demands for intangible, symbolic resources as they do to demands for the incremental allocation of tangible and material resources. Thus for approximately 100 years, the "separate but equal" doctrine in public education was the pluralists' yardstick in the allocation of tangible resources to southern school districts. A new $2-million black grade school was constructed simultaneously with a new $2-million white grade school. Both represented allocations of equal and tangible values which could be objectively measured. In some instances, white students continued to attend a 50-year-old high school even after a brand new black high school had been built. In this instance, again, the tangible measurement of an objective reality clearly indicated a net gain for the black community.

In the allocation of intangible resources which could only be subjectively defined, the pluralists have assumed an attitude of indifference and irrelevance. A clearly demonstrated need for a new black school building could be satisfied by the allocation of tangible resources. This represented an appropriate function of the pluralist political process. But the allocation of intangible, subjectively defined resources represented a totally inappropriate function in the pluralists's view. An education could be provided in the form of schools, teachers, books, and so forth. Equal rights before the law could not be provided in any comparable, tangible form. Human dignity could not be politically or administratively mandated. Due process of the law required the allocation of judicial "resources," not legislative or administrative resources. The long-term consequences of the application of this strategy was a steady compounding of losses for the blacks in the intangible, subjective values of human dignity and individual self-fulfillment.

Anxiety of this type—as opposed to the strain of anxiety stemming from the need for technical and logistical solutions—has been drastically stimulated as a result of the increasing need for solutions to the basic sociopolitical and ethical problems generated in a complex, advanced, industrialized society. At the beginning of the 1960s, the black movement in America was following a clearly defined course in demand of solutions to the basic intangibles involved in a broad set of sociopolitical and ethical problems. At the beginning of the 1970s, similar demands were being made by other chronic losers in the strategy of games—the very young, the very old, the urban poor, the rural migrant, the consumer, the environmentalist, and, of course, the antiwar protestor. Each in his own way had accumulated substantial losses over the years, losses that finally came out from behind the façade of pluralist tranquility as demands for a wide range of highly subjective and intangible responses to an equally complex set of pressing sociopolitical and ethical problems. These demands together with the equally pressing demands for effective solutions to ever-increasing technical and logistical problems, have created a whole new set of relationships— or more precisely, a whole new set of rules—between the pluralist political system and its external environment, the body politic.

In short, turbulence has grown steadily in the environment of the administrative system in recent years and will continue to grow in the foreseeable future. From all indications, it will continue to reveal the pluralist political system as an insufficient and irrelevant political-administrative mechanism.

### The Surge of Turbulence

Technological advances in communications and transportation have reduced the nation to one vast "neighborhood" of subcommunities, and expanding political conflict from a local to a national level. A citizen's anxieties are neither lessened nor fundamentally altered by moving from New York City to Los Angeles or to any other major metropolitan area in the United States today. Crime, traffic congestion, air pollution, substandard housing, inadequate public educational facilities, ghetto poverty, racial inequities have all become national problems which form a common cause for anxiety for approximately 75 percent of the nation's population; and from these problems there appears to be virtually no escape.

The communications networks throughout the nation have contributed to the strongly felt need among the body politic for more of the intangible and symbolic rewards that enhance the quality of life. Many of the gross, tangible socioeconomic disparities in our nation have been dramatically accentuated by the nationwide communications industry. More importantly, however, the industry—especially television—has forcefully demonstrated the needs of underprivileged groups for the intangible and symbolic rewards necessary to eliminate the deeply rooted feelings of a loss of individual identity, to restore the feeling of the intrinsic worth of the individual, to counteract the growing impersonality of an advanced, industrialized society, and to compensate for the frustrations of unsuccessful efforts to effect wide-scale participation in the democratic decision-making process.

Aside from becoming a highly mobile and virtually instantaneously informed society, the bulk of the population is growing younger, receiving more formal education, becoming more affluent and less regimented than ever before. Nevertheless urban life grows more dismal daily, and advances in science and technology, spurred by the application of computer technology, can now effect fundamental change across the span of a decade that earlier would have required a century. Lead time—always a critical element in any decision-making process—has now become drastically telescoped until nearly instantaneous responses are required in answer to a constant stream of challenging events. Increasingly one is caught in a violent surge of the future turning into the past with only a pause at the present.

In this turbulent setting, dynamic interaction between formal public and private organizational units continues; but it continues in an environment that itself has become a principal generator of dynamic change. For example, individuals deprived of the basic intangible and symbolic rewards discussed above are, to an increasing extent, fulfilling those needs in a manner totally independent of the values and attitudes of traditional public and private organizations. Cesar Chavez called for a national boycott of California grapes and a chain reaction started which involved not only a wide variety of individuals and groups, but also a wide variety of related issues. The grape strike effected many different kinds of changes, but most importantly it demonstrated that clusterings of diverse individuals and groups can effectively work around public and private organizations that continue to view demands for change in only tangible and material terms.

As the environment changes fundamentally, decision-making

strategy for public and private organizations becomes engulfed in increasing uncertainty. In an environment of dynamic and constant change, the absence of reliable data on which competitive strategies may be based strips the pluralist system of its balance and order. As the degree of turbulence increases, the competitive nature of the relationships between organizations is substantially modified until relationships between the organizations themselves and between the organizations and the environment all become integrally related. As turbulence increases, the fates of all organizations and their environment become mutually dependent. For example, the actions by General Motors in adding a black minister, the Reverend Leon Sullivan, to its board of directors, and by IBM in adding a black lawyer, Mrs. Patricia Roberts Harris, to its board provide one indication of how an organization may develop a mutually dependent relationship with various elements in its immediate environment.

Another factor that has contributed substantially to the acceleration of environmental turbulence—for our purposes, possibly the central factor—has been the way the executive branch itself has responded to demands for drastic, even radical, change. One must bear in mind that as the current turbulence manifests itself in demands for technical and logistical and sociopolitical and ethical change, the principal (but by no means exclusive) institutions to which such demands are directed are the administrative system of of the government. Clearly these demands for change focus specifically on the allocative and control processes of decision-making of the pluralist-bargaining-incremental system.

Faced with such demands from an increasingly turbulent environment, and caught within an organizational structure that has been specifically designed to impede drastic and rapid change, executive-branch officials appear progressively less responsive the more they try to respond to these demands for change. As noted in previous chapters, the federal bureaucratic structure is a uniquely fashioned device. Stability *and* flexibility, continuity *and* change, deliberation *and* dispatch can each be provided in appropriate circumstances. Despite a statutory limitation of 80 acres of federally owned land that could be leased for private recreational development, plans were devised in 1965–66 by the U.S. Forest Service to provide the Walt Disney Corporation with approximately 300 acres in the Sequoia National Forest for the purposes of developing a year-round recreational resort.[5] Despite the absence of any precedent, and furthermore, despite its mammoth fiscal commitment to the maintenance of United States involvement in Vietnam and Cambodia, the Department of Defense was prepared to underwrite a $200-million loan in an effort to save the Penn Central Railroad from bankruptcy until political events forced a last-minute cancellation of the proposed agreement. Despite disclaimers to the contrary, it was the Department of Defense that responded with amazing dispatch and demonstrated extreme administrative agility in shipping 2.5 million pounds of grapes to our troops in Vietnam just when the consequences of the national boycott of California grapes were beginning to be felt by the owners. In other words, for those who knew their way through the political labyrinth, those who knew how to play the Great Game, and abided by its rules, change was possible. The politically expedient face of bureaucracy could always be made to smile if one knew where to find the funnybone. The uninitiated, the amateur advocates, especially those who sought intangible, subjectively defined, symbolic rewards encountered an entirely different image of bureaucracy which bore a striking resemblance to the grim countenance of Max Weber. When the occasion demanded, the rigid impersonality of bureaucracy could be effectively transmitted through the inflexible enforcement of standard operating procedures. This practice was normally quite adequate in disarming the unprofessional sorties on the pluralist public policy machine that occasionally charged forth from an otherwise relatively stable and predictable environment.

As a short-term defense mechanism the bland impersonality of bureaucratic rigidity can be viewed as an extremely effective device which can be used to undercut "improperly" presented demands for change. Unfortunately, those who have encountered this image of bureaucracy most frequently have been the effectively disenfranchised citizens; they have sought simple solutions to basic problems that required instead a highly personalized, imaginative, and flexible application of the bureaucratic structure. These individuals have rejected the image of public bureaucracy as an effective, equitable, and responsive problem-solving mechanism. In long-range terms, the application of the rigid, impersonal side of the executive bureaucracy has resulted in a steady compilation of perceived losses by an expanding segment of the body politic; such losses can never be offset by any subsequent incremental gains as long as the allocation and control processes are maintained within the same structural framework.

## Structural Rigidity

The rejection of the public bureaucracy as an equitable and responsive problem-solving mechanism by a growing segment of the body politic represents a key element in the mounting environmental turbulence. The focus of the administrative structure within the pluralist political process at home is not unlike the posture assumed by many administrators in connection with the nature of our policies abroad, especially those aimed at the emerging new nations. For both foreign and domestic purposes, pluralist administrators have been intent on maintaining the myth that political development, for nations as well as groups and individuals, has been simply a function of technical and structural modernization. As a result, for nearly two decades the pluralist administrative structure has assumed a posture which has been highly publicized in the name of innovative change, but which, in actual practice, has done nothing more than replace old techniques, structures, and equipment with modern, tangible devices. Especially within the domestic setting this approach has manifested itself quite clearly in the distribution of tangible, objectively defined resources.

New schools, hospitals, highways, public housing projects, expanded public welfare services, and an induced economic hyperactivity are but a few of the examples that have provided tangible evidence of progress without creating any serious disruption in the pluralist administrative structure. The formula has been delightfully simple: progress without structural change becomes an effective stopgap tactic for shunting off occasional turbulence. But the long-term results of this shortsightedness are all too apparent. The development of an individual as a fully expressive, self-activated citizen is not aided and encouraged merely by a cascading flow of tangible, material resources.

If the object of true political development is to increase the problem-solving capacity of an individual, group, or nation, then an equitable and responsive public bureaucracy must be prepared to allocate both tangible and intangible political resources in the manner best designed to advance the attainment of this ultimate goal. Acting in this capacity and toward this goal, the administrator assumes an invaluable role as a *change agent* in the sociopolitical and ethical development of the individual. If the political and administrative system sees the solution of problems basically in terms of the system's capacity to generate tangible goods and services, or "things," then its orientation is towards inputs. In this context, the administrator assumes the significant role of a *transfer agent* in the maintenance and preservation of system stability.

The transfer agent may indeed recognize the dynamic forces of change that generate environmental turbulence, and he may even become sincerely committed to the validity of many of the demands for change. Unfortunately, however, since the transfer agent is forced to rely on the known and proven strategies of the pluralist political system—the scope of conflict must be contained and its intensity minimized—the more "committed" he becomes, the more irrelevant and inappropriate his strategies appear when directed toward the politics of turbulence. As uncertainty and instability increase, the transfer agent becomes increasingly fixed to his established repertoire of allocative and control responses. This means that demands for change which deviate from the established set of responses are either distorted to fit the standard responses or, worse, completely ignored until their scope and intensity reach potentially catastrophic proportions.

Adaptation to change is directly related to the capacity of the internal mechanisms of any system to integrate the new forces in an orderly and steady fashion. When the rate of change exceeds the capacity of a particular system to integrate or absorb the new forces in an orderly and steady fashion, the system may become overloaded. The overload may, in turn, cause one or more of the internal mechanisms to malfunction. In no small measure do the patterns of urban disorder in the United States reveal the inadequacies of many local governments in adapting to accelerating rates of change. Under these circumstances, either the rate of change must be decreased, or the structure of the system must be altered to increase its capacity to absorb the accelerated rates of change in an orderly and steady fashion.

Committed pluralists reject the alternative of changing the system's structural capacity to absorb change and the speed with which it can do so; they are content, instead, to ride out the storm of turbulence until it dissipates itself. In large part, therefore, environmental turbulence is the result of the structural characteristics of the pluralists' administrative system. Given the manner in which they have responded to environmental turbulence and demands for change, it seems clear that new administrative structures must be devised if increasing demands for change are to be integrated in a manageable and tolerable manner. The transfer agent of the pluralist system, for example, is a product of the system structure; but it is the need for trained change agents that grows steadily. Effective change agents cannot possibly emerge until basic alterations are made in the internal mechanisms of the system. The future of an effective, equitable, and responsive administrative system is contingent upon the extent to which these changes are effected.

## Chapter VI

# THE FUTURE OF
# ADMINISTRATION

The danger of the internal structural mechanisms of any system breaking down is by no means purely academic. As the rate of change increases, organizations situated in the center of the current of change are unavoidably affected. If such organizations cannot adjust their internal mechanisms to absorb the change, the probability of organizational collapse is high. Numerous examples of the collapse of vast, complex business and financial structures could be cited. The old European cartels, the pre-1929 American interlocking corporate directorates, and, currently, such conglomerates as Penn Central and Link-Temco-Vought provide dramatic illustrations of how inability to respond to external change can have disastrous results. In an increasingly interrelated and interdependent world, the system overload and subsequent breakdown of component organizations inevitably add stresses on many other components of the system. The collapse of the Penn Central Railroad was borne heavily by other railroads, its investors, and the federal government. For one of its investors especially—the University of Pennsylvania—the shock waves from the collapse of the company created severe stress within its own organization. Penn Central represented the university's second largest stock holding, totalling approximately 4 percent of its common stock portfolio. This was a total allocation of more than $4,000,000 of the university's endowment funds. When the telltale signs of the railroad's impending disaster finally surfaced in May 1970, the university's investment advisors moved as quickly as possible to unload more than 90,000 shares of Penn Central stock controlled by the university. In five trading days all of the shares were sold at an average price of $12.25 per share. The net loss to the university's endowment fund was slightly more than $3 million.[1]

Like private corporations, government agencies conduct their affairs in a way that directly affects the psychic and physical well-being of millions of Americans—individuals whose investment of confidence in return for security will be directly affected by the public organization's capacity to respond to rapid change effectively and equitably. The discussion throughout the previous chapters has stressed that organizational adaptation to change is directly related to how the allocative and control structures are developed. The pluralist-incremental and rational-comprehensive models represent distinct contrasts in structures for allocation and control. The inability of the pluralist system to absorb rapid change effectively is painfully apparent. This question then remains: Insofar as a projected future of increased technological complexity and increased sociopolitical turbulence are concerned, are the allocative and control structures of the rational-comprehensive approach capable of sustaining accelerated rates of change? Is this model capable of providing the tangible and intangible sustenance for the full political development of the individual in a postindustrial age?

## The Range of Alternatives

One way of approaching this question is to examine the various alternatives that are available. For example, one may consider that the control function in any organization may be either centralized in the hands of a few top-level executive officials or decentralized among many middle- and lower-level executive officials. Likewise, the allocative function—viewed in most simplistic terms—may be either incrementally or nonincrementally administered. In relating these two functions to each other, four possible alternatives emerge as indicated in Figure 2, page 94.

The first alternative, Type I, represents the traditional pluralist-bargaining-incremental model; the limitations of its decentralized control structure and its incremental allocative structure in func-

Figure 2

ALTERNATIVE STRUCTURES

CONTROL STRUCTURE

|  | | Decentralized | Centralized |
|---|---|---|---|
| **ALLOCATIVE STRUCTURES** | *Incremental* | TYPE I | TYPE II |
| | *Nonincremental* | TYPE IV | TYPE III |

tioning effectively in the face of rapid and complex sociopolitical change have been discussed in detail. It does not represent a viable alternative as the innovative, change-oriented mechanism of the future. The differences between Types I and II are significant. The latter would centralize authority and power in contrast to the highly fragmented pattern of autonomous and semiautonomous administrative subunits characteristic of the pluralist system. Yet as long as top-level executive officials in this centralized control model would be committed to the incremental allocation of resources, adaptation to change could be expected to follow a consolidative course rather than an innovative one.

A commitment to innovative adaptation and the anticipation of change could be accomplished within the context of the non-incremental and centralized model of Type III. The centralized control and nonincremental allocative structures characteristic of this alternative represent the basic framework of the rational-comprehensive approach. That is, it is within this administrative context that rational, long-range scanning could be combined most effectively with comprehensive long-range planning in the development of program alternatives. Type IV represents an administrative model which would set a nonincremental allocative structure within a decentralized control context. In other words, this model suggests a pattern of autonomous and semiautonomous administrative units each applying the analytical techniques of the rational-comprehensive allocation of resources in their respective spheres. In such a system, innovative responses and the anticipation of change would be, at least, theoretically conceivable.

In practice, however, serious dysfunctions could develop within a Type-IV model. Structured as it is to maximize discretion in policy programming, the model significantly lacks overall coordination of effort and broad policy direction and focus—despite the analytical framework in which decisions would be made. The advantages gained by placing the allocative structure within an analytical framework might be more than offset if a decentralized and fragmented control structure were retained. This dilemma could theoretically be surmounted most effectively by the pure rational-comprehensive model (Type III). This prospect, however, disturbs many persons who envision a vast citizenry lockstepping in unison with a Gosplan of the future.

### The Policy Analyst

As long as the search for alternative administrative futures is fixed on securing operating effectiveness, sociopolitical equity, or bureaucratic responsiveness, the ability of the political system to develop broad-scale, innovative, and anticipatory mechanisms of change within a rapidly changing and complex environment will diminish dramatically. Effective, equitable, and relevant administrative responses must be developed within a structural context that can maintain a centralized overall policy focus, an analytically devised set of program alternatives, a high degree of practical operating discretion and flexibility, and a strong orientation towards ethical values. An administrative system must increase and extend the range of choices men can make, and not dictate what choices they have to make. The development of these choices must be designed to enhance each individual's ability to overcome the technical and logistical, sociopolitical and ethical conflicts generated in a turbulent environment. And finally, the administrative structure must be designed to insure that the development and extension of alternative choices is aggressively pursued on both the national and subnational levels. In short, efforts must be made to develop an administrative structure along the lines of the Type-IV model described above.

Such an approach introduces a series of administrative changes —structural as well as philosophical—which deviate significantly from Weber's traditional bureaucratic model and our own uniquely designed pluralist-incremental hybrid. The administrative future being projected here is designed to increase the overall planning and programming functions of a nationally oriented cadre of administrative specialists skilled in policy analysis. On these individuals must fall the responsibility of applying the full range of systems analysis to the broad-scale public policy process. In this context, top-level executive officials, including the President, assume positions of critical importance. They must learn how to guide and direct these policy analysts to enhance the qualitative level of the public policy process. It is patently unrealistic, however, to assume that such executive leadership will burst forth spontaneously. Effective guidance and direction of policy analysts will depend on the extent to which top-level executive officials have direct access to accurate and relevant data concerning the forces of change in the environment.

To supply executives with the facts they must have, the information network characteristic of the traditional bureaucratic model will not suffice. One of the primary functions of a hierarchical structure is to eliminate or consolidate information inputs as they progress upward through the various organizational echelons. While an extensive amount of data enters into the base of the organization's inverted communications funnel, the hierarchical structure provides a built-in filtering process which can effectively screen out most of this data before it ever reaches the apex of the pyramid. Within a highly stable system this type of communications channel, while not without its pitfalls, does not normally produce disastrous miscalculations. In a changing and complex environment, uncertainty and ambiguity are drastically compounded, and to process information from this type of environmental setting in the normal, filtering fashion is to run the risk of gross distortion. If policy analysts are to follow a relevant, reliable, and responsive course, top-level executive officials must have access to reliable information concerning the forces of change within the environment. As one organizational theorist has noted:

> It seems important to distinguish energic inputs and outputs from informational ones. Energic inputs include machinery, personnel, clientele in the case of service organizations, electric power, and so on. Informational inputs are not well conceptualized although there is no doubt of their increasing importance in environments which are more complex and changeable. . . .
>
> The importance of communication for organizational change has been stressed by Ohlin, March and Simon, Benne, Lippitt, and others. Diversity of informational input has been used to explain the creativity of individuals as well as social systems. The importance of boundary positions as primary

sources of innovative inputs from the environment has been stressed by March and Simon, and by Kahn *et al.* James Miller hypothesizes that up to a maximum, which no living system has yet reached, *the more energy a system devotes to information processing (as opposed to productive and maintenance activity) the more likely the system is to survive.*[2]

Specifically, what is needed is a second group of highly trained administrative specialists, a cadre of professional change agents, who, being strategically placed in boundary-spanning units, would have direct, face-to-face contact with individuals and groups in the turbulent environment, and, in addition, would have direct contact with top-level executive officials and their policy analysts.

## Boundary-Spanning Units

The change agent and the boundary-spanning unit are two concepts that assume major importance in the Type-IV administrative structure being projected here. The boundary-spanning units may be viewed as those administrative units of any organization which come in direct, face-to-face contact with forces in the external environment that are either directly or indirectly affected by the implementation of the organization's policies and programs. For the purposes of this discussion, a boundary may be drawn between the formal apparatus of the federal government (the executive, legislative, and judicial branches) and the rest of the nation's society (the body politic). A secondary boundary may be drawn separating the three branches of government from each other. Thus the external environment of the executive branch includes the body politic as well as the legislative and judicial branches. Obviously the future of any executive administrative system will depend on the relationships that are formed between the executive branch and the legislative and judicial systems. The critical importance of the relationships especially between the executive and legislative systems has been stressed throughout the previous chapters: an extended analysis of the future of such relationships must be conducted elsewhere. Thus the discussion that follows here focuses on the projected relationships between the executive branch and the nongovernmental forces in its external environment.

In this case, the boundary-spanning units of the executive branch are the administrative units that are situated directly on the boundary dividing the formal bureaucratic apparatus from the body politic. In traditional terms this distinction could be clearly drawn between the administrative unit and its specific clientele group. Thus for the Department of Agriculture the boundary-spanning units which came in direct, face-to-face contact with farmers were the county agents' offices; for the Justice Department, as Cesar Chavez discovered, The Bureau of Immigration and Naturalization held this position; for the Treasury Department, local Internal Revenue Service offices served this purpose. In the pluralist political context, however, given a highly stable external environment, these lowest-echelon administrative units assumed a function that more properly could be characterized as boundary-guarding rather than boundary-spanning. Their primary responsibility was to guard against any attempted improper intrusion into the pluralist political process. Their effectiveness in this regard has already been discussed, as has their general ineffectiveness in a turbulent environment. As the environment has become unstable, the need for boundary-spanning rather than boundary-guarding units has become essential for the effective continuance of administration by the executive branch.

The boundary-spanning units can be viewed as being composed of highly specialized work teams, situated within the segment of the environment that is directly or indirectly affected by the policies and programs of the executive departments, agencies, or commissions. The Interior Department, which has jurisdiction over the protection and maintenance of the nation's public lands and natural resources, including offshore oil deposits, was satisfied with its administrative effectiveness when its boundary-guarding units received, reviewed, and approved or disapproved bids from private oil companies to drill for offshore oil. Now, however, these units are besieged with protests from conservation groups, homeowner groups, fishing, boating, and recreational groups, municipal governments, state governments, and, of course, the private oil companies. The boundary-guarding units, in short, have become totally ineffective in developing meaningful interacting and interdependent relationships between the Interior Department and this segment of its turbulent environment. It is this function that the boundary-spanning units are intended to accomplish, and their effectiveness, of course, depends on the success of the work teams that are assigned to each of these units. The members of these work teams are to be viewed as highly skilled administrative *generalists* whose primary task is to link their respective organizations into a particular segment of the turbulent environment—to span the boundary between the organization and the environment in a meaningful, purposeful, and relevant manner. As public administrators these individuals assume essential positions in the Type-IV administrative system being proposed here; as professional agents of change they assume a critical role in establishing the executive branch as an effective, responsive *and* equitable problem-solving structure.

## The Change Agent

As stated before, the difference between transfer agents and change agents is significant. Transfer agents are primarily concerned with the transfer of tangible and material resources from the government to the body politic; the basic premise of the transfer theory is that political development is directly related to the manipulation of the symbols of modernity. Change agents, on the other hand, are committed to the premise that political development is a direct consequence of an increase in the problem-solving ability of the individual situated in the external environment.

Specifically, this means that the change agents must become a part of the changing setting in their operations, their location, and the range of their interpersonal relationships. They must become self-consciously involved in the complexity of the moment if they are to be at all effective in turning the forces of change within their respective environments away from violence and destruction. In other words, they must be able to manipulate the full range of tangible and intangible organization resources at their disposal in order to expand rather than limit the range of choices that are open to the individual. The ultimate goal of the change agents is to transform the feelings of political hopelessness and despair (which may ultimately lead in the direction of political violence) into feelings of political meaningfulness and relevance. A high degree of confidence in the ability to control one's own destiny is an essential characteristic of political development. The level of confidence that one reflects in this regard is in part related to the range of choices that are available. In line with the Type-IV model, the critical function of the change agents is to insure that the resources of their respective executive organizations are used to expand rather than limit this range of choice.

In the matter of choice, therefore, ultimate sovereignty must reside with the individual, not the state or one of its administrative units. The administrative units have the primary responsibility of generating purposeful and meaningful choices; the ultimate choice itself, however, becomes the personal and exclusive responsibility of the individual. The most persistent obstacle to true political development is man's own fear of facing the awesome responsibilities of choice. Problem-solving alternatives may be expanded in order to enhance the political development of the individual. But the growth process will surely be stunted unless the individual develops a greater tolerance for ambiguity. The ultimate consequence of the developmental process is that the individual will be called upon to replace the intense anxiety of frustration and alienation with an equally intense anxiety of the freedom of personal choice. It becomes the critical responsibility of the change agents to prove that a life built around choices is infinitely preferable to one without choice. If one can be convinced that the anxiety associated with the ambiguity of choice is a perfectly normal reaction in this highly uncertain age, then the willingness to assume the personal responsibility of choice may increase.

As members of the work teams which staff the boundary-spanning units of executive departments, agencies, and commissions, the change agents must be prepared to assume three essential functions. First, as indicated above, if rational-comprehensive policy analysis by top-level executive officials is to be effective, the need for accurate and pertinent information concerning the environment becomes essential. It is the change agents who gather the data. Even more importantly, however, these generalists must learn to anticipate the environmental forces of change. A key element of the rational-comprehensive approach involves the systematic analysis of the future to detect the emergence of incipient change forces. For the policy analysts this technique may be considered their macro-scanning function—the search for the development of broad-scale, national change movements. For the change agents the same technique may be viewed in terms of a micro-scanning function which seeks to detect future forces of change within a limited, highly specific sociopolitical context. Thus, in the overall formulation of broad-scale public policy, macro- and micro-analyses become essential compliments of each other, and the change agents assume a role that is equal in importance to that of the policy analysts.

The second major function of the change agents is of comparable importance. If the administrative structure of the future is to combine centralized comprehensive planning and programming with decentralized administrative implementation, the change agents must become *the* vital link in this venture. These generalists, working within the broad public policy parameters established by top-level executives and their policy analysts, must devise and invent effective, equitable, and relevant solutions to the pressing technical and logistical and sociopolitical and ethical problems that develop within their specific environmental sectors. It is the change agents who must be permitted, and who must be willing, to utilize the resources of their boundary-spanning units to become an integral part of the turbulent environment. Admittedly this role places a high premium on "unorthodox" administrative behavior. The change agents must be prepared to approach the environmental problems that confront them with a high degree of inventiveness. They must be willing to experiment and to innovate in the search for specific solutions—however tentative and impermanent—to specific problems. They must be able to operate effectively in an atmosphere of high ambiguity and constant flux. They must, in a word, become totally involved in the turbulent current if only to guide it away from a course of destructive violence.

The third major function of these generalists is to impart meaningfulness and relevance to the direction of the public policy process. In the face of increasing environmental complexity and rapid technological change, the change agents stand as the buffer between moral man and immoral society, between the personified citizen and an impersonalized bureaucracy, between rational-comprehensive planning and irrational, disjointed behavior. It is the change agents who must insure that equity enters into the administrative equation, and it is the change agents who must become the principal allocators of the organization's resources so as to strengthen the growth of the intangible, subjectively defined values of the individual. The long-term cumulative effects of individual and group anxiety, frustration, bitterness, and worthlessness must be arrested, and the causes of these effects eliminated. This task falls to the change agents who must introduce the concept of participatory democracy into the administrative process of systematic, rational-comprehensive analysis.

## Internal Organizational Change

In considering the administrative future projected here, it should be apparent that the traditional hierarchical pattern of superior-subordinate, chain-of-command relationships is a totally inappropriate mechanism for maximizing organizational effectiveness, responsiveness, and equity in a turbulent environment. Instead the internal administrative structure must be developed around a web of interacting relationships involving top-level executive officials (including the President), policy analysts, and change agents. The change agents, in turn, must develop a set of viable relationships among the various elements within their respective environmental spheres. Joined together, these patterns of reciprocal exchange and control must be geared to maximize both comprehensive policy-making and operating flexibility. For the public organizations and administrators who misread or misinterpret the extent and nature of this interrelated system of the future, the strategy of games will, unfortunately, continue to prevail. But for those who can perceive the conscious and intended linkage deliberately designed to increase the networks of interdependences, the public organization could assume a dynamic, exciting, innovating quality.

Warren Bennis has written extensively about the necessity to develop new organizational structures which he characterizes as highly adaptive, rapidly changing, temporary systems. Within this context leadership assumes collective and collegial dimensions which stress broad participation in both the control and decision-making functions of the organization. Given the variety and magnitude of problems confronting most organizations today, Bennis considers the traditional hierarchical model of Weber—with its power and authority effectively monopolized at the apex—as obsolete. As seen by Bennis, more and more executive constellations are emerging which rely less on the formal and informal manipulation of organizational "power" implicit in the operating procedures of traditional management practice, and more on the development of an effective, collaborative administrative system which enhances the emergence of true synergistic interpersonal relationships.[3]

The concept of synergy is a significant feature of the organizational theories of Abraham Maslow, a humanistic psychologist. Maslow uses the term *synergy* to refer to the type of interpersonal relationship that results when an individual, in pursuit of his own self-interests, enhances the self-interests of others; or when a person actually enhances his own self-interests by unselfishly pursuing purely altruistic goals.

As a psychologist, Maslow was primarily concerned with developing organizational systems that foster and encourage the intra- and interpersonal movement toward "psychological health." A psychologically healthy environment is conducive to self-actualized behavior, or behavior on the part of the individual which is motivated by a true sense of the importance of one's task, the worthiness of one's efforts, and the pride of one's competency. Given these conditions, the individual will be self-motivated (that is, self-actualized) to develop and maintain a deep interpersonal empathy and a strong professional (or occupational) responsibility. Self-actualized behavior diminishes the need for the organizationally induced motivations common to the traditional hierarchical model;

this situation leads toward a collegial, participative, innovative organizational system.

As a humanist, Maslow's psychological concepts assume a definite ethical content. Man's primary commitment is not to his own organization or his job, but to his fellow man. To be recognized as an individual worthy of human dignity one must be able to recognize this quality in his fellow man; but, paradoxically, one can attain this insight only after he is capable of recognizing his own dignity and worthiness. Thus, again, in seeking one's own self-interests one is unconsciously advancing the interests of others. The Judeo-Christian ethic implicit in Maslow is not all love and peace, however. In discussing authoritarian leadership patterns, for instance, Maslow advised, "The correct thing to do with authoritarians is to take them realistically for the bastards they are and then behave toward them as if they were bastards. This is the only realistic way to treat bastards." It was the suppressive nature of the traditional hierarchical model that Maslow viewed as the primary factor inhibiting the development of a psychologically healthy individual. Enlightened management was the only alternative; and for Maslow the humanist, enlightened management assumed the form of secularized religion.

> Enlightened management is one way of taking religion seriously, profoundly, deeply, and earnestly. Of course for those who define religion just as going to a particular building on Sunday and hearing a particular kind of formula repeated, this is all irrelevant. But for those who define religion not necessarily in terms of the supernatural, or ceremonies, or rituals, or dogmas, but in terms of deep concern with the problems of the human species, with the problems of ethics, of the relationship to nature, of the future of man, etc., then this kind of philosophy translated into the work life, turns out to be very much like the new style of management and of organization.[4]

The ethical content of organizational behavior has been developed thoroughly by another organizational theorist, Robert Golembiewski. In addition to developing an organizational model centered around and dominated by the Judeo-Christian ethic, Golembiewski elsewhere presents a detailed organizational model that incorporates the full range of "enlightened management" principles. The colleague model which he advances breaks sharply from the traditional line-staff dichotomy and focuses instead on the horizontal integration of line-staff units. As seen by Golembiewski the vertical arrangement of personnel according to function inhibits interpersonal communications and thus creates a system resistant to change. To maximize the organization's ability to adapt to change quickly and effectively the colleague model divides the organization horizontally into integrated groups or teams which are assigned full responsibility, authority, and control over the organization's final end product, be it the production of shoes or the implementation of an urban renewal program. The colleague model as presented by Golembiewski offers many advantages over the traditional vertical functional structures, but more importantly it is primarily designed to enhance the development of the kind of self-actualized behavior envisioned by Maslow.[5]

A basic similarity exists between Golembiewski's colleague teams and another, more widely recognized management concept, matrix organizations. Frequently referred to as project organizations, program teams, and task teams, the matrix organization is specifically oriented toward the solution of a particular problem or the completion of a particular task or project. That is to say, when a problem of special or unusual significance develops an organization may respond by creating a special "task force" composed of individuals from various divisions or departments within the organization whose individual skills when fused collectively can expedite the resolution of the problem. Once the problem is solved, however, the matrix organization dissolves and the team members return to their normal duty assignments. Golembiewski's colleague model, on the other hand, assumes a very definite permanent character.

From these and other organizational theorists the literature on administrative humanism, broadly defined, is growing rapidly and reflects an increasing awareness of the need to enhance an organization's internal capacity to respond to the forces of dynamic and complex change in an effective, relevant, and equitable manner. In this regard all organizations, public and private, face a serious challenge, and just as Golembiewski seriously questions the efficacy of the traditional, vertically integrated, line-staff dichotomy within organizations, one can apply his analysis and raise the same questions in connection with another administrative dichotomy which has traditionally segregated public and private organizations.

## The Fusion of Public and Private Administration

The internal stability of all administrative structures, public as well as private, is threatened by environmental turbulence. As demands for change continue to mount within the external environment, the forces behind these demands become less inclined to discriminate between public and private administrative sectors. In the minds of the young, the poor, the oppressed—and, indeed, many of the affluent, well-educated groups as well—"bureaucracy" stands for an obstacle to change regardless of whether that obstacle enjoys public or private status under the law. To maintain an effective, equitable, and responsive attitude in an unstable, complex, highly turbulent environment, all administrative units, public and private, will have to develop a sense of social awareness and a commitment to a high degree of social responsibility. Effective adaptation to increasing environmental turbulence depends upon the level of cooperation that can be achieved between public and private organizations in developing meaningful solutions to pressing environmental demands—which is simply another way of suggesting that the time-honored dichotomy between public and private organizations will continue to appear as an increasingly irrelevant consideration.

In the solution of specific technical and logistical problems, the amalgamation of public and private resources in the formation of temporary, project-oriented, matrix organizations at the boundary-spanning level would appear to be especially fruitful. In many instances, public organizations simply do not have the technical and logistical resources to deal effectively with the complex problems of a postindustrial society. The nation's space program is probably the most dramatic illustration of this point. In the development of this program, the public unit (National Aeronautics and Space Administration) depended extensively on the technical and logistical skills of various segments of the private scientific community (for example, the aeronautics, electronics, and computer industries). The net result was a successful fusion of public and private resources in a cooperative problem-solving approach that neither sector acting alone could have adopted.

For the future of administration, the same type of public-private fusion or amalgamation must occur all along the boundary-spanning continuum if effective solutions are to be devised for the ever-increasing quantity and severity of the technical and logistical problems that have recently developed and will continue to develop. As the nation's population grows, the future holds major technological and logistical challenges in simply providing the basic necessities of life—food, clothing, shelter. Sewage and refuse disposal, as well as power and water supplies, cannot continue to be viewed as problems falling exclusively within the public domain. In each of these areas new scientific advancements are essential if public demands are to be effectively and equitably met. The traditional public units are woefully incapable of devising effective technical and logistical solutions to such problems as low-cost medical care, mass occupational retraining, integrated educational programs, economical high-speed transportation between metropolitan centers, and, of course, pollution control. In each of these areas, and in many more, the primary responsibility of public administrative units must be to prepare the body politic to live comfortably in the permanent impermanence—the persistent turbulence—of the future; to increase rather than decrease the range of choices available to each individual in his search for a meaningful and purposeful life; and to insure that within the context of accelerating technological complexity, the intangible, subjectively defined values of the individual are preserved as significantly integral features of the future society. These three critical responsibilities must be met if one entertains any hope whatever of channelling responses to environmental turbulence in a positive, dynamic, and productive direction. But the future will surely evaporate into the past if public and private administrative resources are not fused into matrix-styled work teams at the boundary-spanning level. This includes the last-mentioned responsibility of insuring a high degree of personal individuality in the midst of accelerating technological change.

## The Public Policy Generalist

The technological competence of the nation's scientific community is truly phenomenal; relatively few technical or logistical problems are totally unsolvable, if viewed solely in the abstract. In reality, however, every technical and logistical solution tends to generate its own set of social, political, and ethical problems. The traditional position of the scientific community has been that in the pursuit of pure, scientific truth, sociopolitical and ethical considerations must be viewed as irrelevant. Similarly, the position assumed by the applied scientists, the technicians, and management officials from the private sector of business and industry has been that while certain political considerations may be recognized as valid constraints on policy decisions, social and ethical considerations must be recognized only when presented in terms of broad and ambiguously defined generalities. Within the public sector, administrators traditionally have openly proclaimed their concern for all three factors, but in actual practice the legacy of Max Weber provides a sterile atmosphere of impersonal operating efficiency for some while the pluralist political tradition counsels political prudence for others. In either case, the sociopolitical and ethical considerations involved in public policy decisions often have been minimized, if not completely ignored. In the future, these traditional attitudes must be significantly altered to the extent that sociopolitical and ethical considerations are routinely reflected in both public and private policy-making processes.

The professional change agents hold the key in converting these propositions from pious platitudes into operating realities. The previous discussion of these individuals was focused exclusively on their role in public organizations. To the extent however, that all organizations are directly affected by environmental turbulence and come to view survival in terms of successful adaptation to a highly unpredictable, impermanent, and complex future, then the role of the change agents becomes critically related to the survival of all organizations, public and private. The change agents become, in the real sense of the word, *the* professional administrators of the future; they represent the key operatives who can complete the linkage of interacting and interdependent relationships between the formal organizations and the turbulent environment, and between the public and private boundary-spanning units. As administrative generalists their basic problem-solving orientation will accentuate their inclination toward innovation, experimentation, and inventiveness.

Within the Type-IV administrative model discussed earlier in this chapter, the role of the change agents cannot be viewed apart from the role of the policy analysts. The change agents must develop and apply their interpersonal skills within a goal-oriented framework established by the analysts and top-level policy officials. Conversely, an essential input in the formulation of goals must be provided by the change agents in the form of objective data and program evaluations. In short, if the organization hopes to respond to the forces of complex change in an effective, responsive, and equitable manner—if it is to make any attempt to respond to the technical and logistical needs of its relevant environment in a sociopolitical and ethical manner—it must combine planning and innovation, comprehensive programs and discretionary implementation, routine anticipatory scanning of the future and routine administrative inventiveness for the present.

To achieve this kind of organizational "mix" between policy analysts and change agents, the ideas of Golembiewski, Bennis, Maslow and others must be applied. For example, if one is inclined to accept the notions of colleague teams, horizontal integration, role exchange, temporary problem-solving projects, and sustaining, self-actualized program groups, then the traditional bureaucratic hang-ups of rank, status, power, chain of command, line versus staff, policy versus administration, and public versus private sectors all can be viewed from an entirely different perspective.

Given the growing complexity of technological and sociopolitical change, the natural tendency is for individuals and organizations to develop increasingly narrow occupational and professional specializations. In many instances this pattern will not only be inevitable but absolutely necessary. For example, research in genetic structure, which holds many of the secrets of life itself, must continue to depend on the efforts of highly trained scientists—the "superspecialists." However, in the formulation and implementation of public policy, the tendency toward superspecialization should be limited. If the primary concern of public and private organizations is to meet the present and future technical and logistical needs of the body politic in a thoroughly responsible sociopolitical and ethical fashion, then the concept of specialization must become situationally defined along the constantly changing continuum of interacting forces. If the Type-IV administrative model suggested here is to prove viable, the policy analysts must think and act like macro-change agents and the change agents must similarly behave as micro-analysts. In the public policy area, the critical need of the future would seem to be the development of "supergeneralists."

Realistically, of course, the inclination to move in the opposite direction is equally compelling. For many, the strength of America is directly dependent upon the maintenance of our technical superiority. As noted by one congressman during the debates on the SST program, "America cannot be the most advanced nation in the world . . . without the economic strength which comes in our capacity to do things better, quicker, and cheaper. The SST is such an economic advantage for our nation in the world. . . ." If the spirit of this sentiment is accepted, the formulation and conduct of public policy must inevitably move in the direction of "superspecialization." This concluding chapter has attempted to caution against a move in that direction and to suggest a reasonable alternative to both the bargaining-incremental and the rational-comprehensive models of public administration.

# Notes

CHAPTER I

1. W. H. Auden, "Law like Love," *The Collected Poetry of W. H. Auden* (New York: Random House, Inc., 1945), p. 75. Used by permission.
2. The National Labor Relations Act, commonly referred to as the Wagner Act, required employers to recognize labor unions and to engage in collective bargaining with legitimately elected labor union representatives. The Act created the National Labor Relations Board, which was empowered to conduct and certify representation elections when two or more unions claimed to represent workers, to investigate employee claims of unfair labor practices, and to issue cease and desist orders. The scope of the act was limited to employees who were "substantially" and directly engaged in interstate commerce. Given the traditional nature of agriculture techniques, farm workers (and especially migratory field workers) have been excluded from NLRA jurisdiction. As a result of advanced technology, increased farm mechanization, and the growth of conglomerate business organizations, this traditional conception of farm labor is becoming increasingly strained. Currently efforts are being pursued in both the executive branch and in Congress to include farm labor under the provisions of either existing or new federal legislation.
3. U.S. House of Representatives, Education and Labor Special Subcommittee on Labor, *Hearings,* 91st Cong., 1st sess., 16–17 July 1969.
4. *Congressional Record,* 113, Part 14, 90th Cong., 1st sess., 1967, 18870–80.
5. "Westlands Water District Contract," *Hearings,* U.S. House of Representatives, Committee on Interior and Insular Affairs, 88th Cong., 2nd sess., 1964, p. 78.
6. *Ibid.,* p. 71.
7. *New York Times,* 27 June 1969, p. 17.
8. *Idem.*
9. U.S. Senate, Labor and Public Welfare Subcommittee on Migratory Labor, *Hearings,* 1st Cong., 1st sess., 29 September 1969.
10. *Ibid.,* 1 August 1969.
11. *New York Times,* 1 May 1970, p. 31.

12. Paul Diesing, *Reason in Society*, (Urbana: University of Illinois Press, 1962), pp. 198, 203–4. (Italics added.)
13. For example, see the writings of Walter Berns, Wallace Mendelson, Rocco Tresolini, and Paul Bartholomew.
14. Louis C. Gawthrop, *Administrative Practice and Democratic Theory* (Boston: Houghton Mifflin Company, 1970).
15. Richard Harris, *Justice: The Crisis of Law, Order, and Freedom in America*, (New York: E. P. Dutton & Co., Inc., 1970).
16. See Francis Russell, *The Shadow of Blooming Grove*, (New York: McGraw-Hill Book Company, 1968).
17. Binghamton (N. Y.) *Press*, 2 March 1970, p. 10A. Syndicated by *The Chicago Sun-Times*.
18. *Conduct of National Security Policy*, U.S. Senate, Government Operations Subcommittee on National Security and International Operations, 89th Cong., 1st sess., 1965, Part 3, p. 121.
19. Charles Lindblom, "The Science of Muddling Through," *Public Administration Review*, **19** (Spring 1959), 84.
20. The writings of Charles Lindblom, Robert Dahl, and Lester Milbrath, for example, reflect this attitude.
21. Charles Lindblom and David Braybrooke, *A Strategy of Decision* (New York: The Free Press, 1963), p. 190.
22. *Ibid.*, p. 74.
23. *Ibid.*, p. 122.
24. "A Critique of the Elitist Theory of Democracy," *American Political Science Review*, **60**, (June 1966), 285. Walker's critique is aimed at incremental theory, which he prefers to designate as an elitist theory of democracy. Although the elitist overtones in the pluralist-bargaining-incremental approach can be detected, the concept of elitism when applied to the pluralist-bargaining-incremental scheme does not conform to my own general notions of a traditionally elitist system. This is in no way intended to detract from the excellent critique presented by Walker; I simply prefer to designate the advocates of the P-B-I approach as "incrementalists." (See Chapter Three.)

## CHAPTER II

1. See Woodrow Wilson, "The Study of Public Administration," *Political Science Quarterly*, **2** (1887), 197-222; Frank Goodnow, *Politics and Administration* (New York: The Macmillan Company, 1900); Leonard D. White, *Introduction to the Study of Public Administration*, (New York: The Macmillan Company, 1926); and F. W. Willoughby, *Principles of Public Administration* (Baltimore: The Johns Hopkins Press, 1927).
2. Presidential Executive Order of 25 August 1965.
3. *Planning-Programming-Budgeting: Initial Memorandum*, U.S. Senate, Government Operations Subcommittee on National Security and International Affairs, Committee Print, 90th Cong., 1st sess., 1967, p. 8.
4. Richard Neustadt, *Presidential Power* (New York: John Wiley & Sons, 1960).
5. For example, see Raymond Bauer, Ithiel de Sola Pool, and Lewis Dexter, *American Business and Public Policy* (New York: Atherton Press, Inc., 1963).
6. An excellent study of executive behavior and administrative accountability in a democratic society is presented by Frederick Mosher, *Democracy and The Public Service* (New York: Oxford University Press, 1968).

7. *Congressional Quarterly Weekly Report,* **28**, No. 13 (27 March 1970), 858–59.

## CHAPTER III

1. Frank R. Kent, *The Great Game of Politics* (New York: Doubleday, Doran & Co., 1931) pp. 29, 31.
2. H. L. Mencken, *A Mencken Chrestomathy* (New York: Alfred A. Knopf, 1953), p. 168.
3. Marshall and Gladys Dimock, *Public Administration,* 3rd ed. (New York: Holt, Rinehart and Winston, Inc., 1964), p. 104.
4. Harold Stein (ed.), *Public Administration and Policy Development* (New York: Harcourt, Brace, Jovanovich, 1952), p. xvi.
5. John Kenneth Galbraith, *American Capitalism: The Theory of Countervailing Power* (Boston: Houghton Mifflin Company, 1952).
6. For an explanatory essay of this philosophy and an extensive bibliography of its adherents (who have joined together to form the Public Choice Society) see Vincent and Elinor Ostrom, "Public Choice: A Different Approach to the Study of Public Administration," *Public Administration Review,* **31**, No. 2 (1971), 203–16.
7. T. Harry Williams, *Huey Long* (New York: Alfred A. Knopf, Inc., 1970), p. 767.
8. This tactic forms the basis of James Madison's pluralism as outlined in his *Federalist No. 10.* See also Gawthrop, *Administrative Practice and Democratic Theory,* pp. 67–74.
9. Jack Walker, "A Critique of the Elitist Theory of Democracy," *loc. cit.*
10. "The Polls," *Public Opinion Quarterly,* **33** (Spring 1969), 148–52.

## CHAPTER IV

1. David Halberstam, "The Programming of Robert McNamara," *Harpers,* February 1971, p. 37.
2. Elizabeth Drew, "HEW Grapples With PPBS," *The Public Interest,* Summer 1967, pp. 9–29.
3. Stuart H. Loory, "Nixon Bridle Binds Aide's Run to Academic Freedom," A Gannett News Service Special, The Binghamton (N. Y.) *Sunday Press,* 19 July 1970, p. 1C.
4. Diesing, *Reason in Society.*
5. See David Novick (ed.), *Program Budgeting: Program Analysis and the Federal Budget* (Cambridge, Mass.: Harvard University Press, 1965); Fremont Lyden and Ernest Miller (eds.), *Planning-Programming-Budgeting* (Chicago: Markham Publishing Co., 1967); Harvey Hinrichs and Graeme Taylor, *Program Budgeting and Cost Benefit Analysis* (Pacific Palisades, Calif.: Goodyear Publishing Co., Inc., 1969); Robert Haveman and Julius Margolis (eds.), *Public Expenditures and Policy Analysis* (Chicago, Markam Publishing Co., 1970).
6. Aaron Wildavsky, "The Political Economy of Efficiency," *Public Administration Review,* **24**, No. 4 (December 1966).
7. For example see Charles Hitch and Roland McKean, *The Economics of Defense in the Nuclear Age* (New York: Atheneum Publishers, 1965); Robert Art, *The TFX Decision: McNamara and the Military* (Boston: Little, Brown, and Company, 1968).
8. Aaron Wildavsky and Arthur Hammann, "Comprehensive Versus Incremental Budgeting in the Department of Agriculture," in *Planning-Programming-Budgeting: A Systems Approach to Management,* Fremont Lyden and Ernest Miller (eds.) (Chicago: Markham Publishing Co., 1967).

9. William Gorham, "Notes of a Practitioner," *The Public Interest,* No. 8 (Summer 1967), 4.
10. Frederick Mosher and John Harr, *Programming Systems and Foreign Affairs Leadership* (New York: Oxford University Press, 1970).
11. *Ibid.,* p. 37.
12. See for example Aaron Wildavsky, *The Politics of the Budgetary Process,* (Boston: Little, Brown and Company, 1964); Richard Fenno, *The Power of the Purse* (Boston: Little, Brown and Company, 1966).
13. U.S. House of Representatives, Committee on Foreign Affairs, "Foreign Assistance Act of 1964," *Hearings,* 88th Cong., 2nd sess., 1964, p. 8. (Italics added.)
14. U.S. House of Representatives, Appropriations Subcommittee on Foreign Operations, "Foreign Aid Appropriations for 1965," *Hearings,* 88th Cong., 2nd sess., 1964, Part I, p. 356.
15. U.S. House of Representatives, Committee on Foreign Affairs, *op. cit.,* pp. 103, 104.
16. William M. Capron, "The Impact of Analysis on Bargaining in Government," in Louis C. Gawthrop, *Administrative Practice and Democratic Theory.*
17. Mosher and Harr, *op. cit.,* p. 239.
18. Wildavsky, "The Political Economy of Efficiency," pp. 304–5.

## CHAPTER V

1. *New York Times,* 12 May 1969, p. 26.
2. *Ibid.,* 25 June 1970, p. 26.
3. John Noble Wilford, "Price of Technology," *Ibid.,* 31 July 1970, p. 34.
4. Robert Michels, *Political Parties* (New York: Collier Books, 1962), p. 368.
5. *New York Times,* 9 June 1969, p. 38; *Congressional Quarterly Weekly Report,* **28,** No. 23 (5 June 1970), 1503. The plan was temporarily halted when the Sierra Club obtained a court injunction in July 1969. The injunction decision, however, was reversed in September 1970 by the Ninth Circuit U.S. Court of Appeals. The Sierra Club plans to appeal the decision. See *New York Times,* 20 September 1970, p. 61.

## CHAPTER VI

1. J. A. Livingston, syndicated column appearing in the Binghamton (N. Y.) *Evening Press,* 29 June 1970, p. 1C.
2. Shirley Terreberry, "The Evolution of Organizational Environments," *Administrative Science Quarterly,* **12** (March 1968), 608, 609–10. (Italics added.)
3. See especially Warren Bennis, *Changing Organizations* (New York: McGraw-Hill Book Company, 1966); and Warren Bennis and Philip Slater, *The Temporary Society* (New York: Harper & Row, Publishers, 1968).
4. Abraham Maslow, *Eupsychian Management* (Homewood, Ill., Richard D. Irwin and The Dorsey Press, 1965), p. 62. The general character of Maslow's humanism can be gained from *Eupsychian Management,* which also provides a relatively complete bibliography of Maslow's writings.
5. See especially Robert Golembiewski, *Men, Management, and Morality* (New York: McGraw-Hill Book Company, 1965); and *Organizing Men and Power* (Chicago: Rand McNally & Co., 1967).

# Bibliography

## CHAPTER I

The California grape strike incident serves as an excellent case study of the complexity of our federal governmental system. Public policy issues, in this case the grape strike, frequently provide a valuable overall view of the political system which cannot be gained from a survey of more general considerations, in this case the migratory labor question. For example, Robert J. Art, *The TFX Decision* (Boston: Little, Brown and Company, 1968) analyzes the many ramifications of a major decision made by former Secretary of Defense Robert McNamara. James W. Davis, Jr., and Kenneth M. Dolbeare provide an overview of the political system in their *Little Groups of Neighbors: The Selective Service System* (Chicago: Markham Publishing Company, 1968). John D. Donovan, *The Politics of Poverty* (New York: Pegasus, 1967) is an excellent case study of the complexity and confusion that frequently characterize the policy process in general. Eugene Feingold's *Medicare: Policy and Politics* (San Francisco: Chandler Publishing Company, 1966) provides a detailed policy analysis of the medical assistance issues along with extensive bibliographies on various aspects of the issue. James L. Sundquist, *Politics and Policy* (Washington: The Brookings Institution, 1968) examines the development of major domestic public policy issues from 1953 through 1966; although this study focuses on the legislative branch, it can provide a helpful supplemental view of the public policy process.

## CHAPTER II

The literature on the structural and functional characteristics of the executive branch is extensive and reveals a rich diversity of viewpoints.

Starting with Woodrow Wilson's classic article, "The Study of Public Administration" (*Political Science Quarterly* 2, 1887), the theme of the dichotomy between politics and administration is advanced to its fullest elaboration in Luther Gulick, et al., *Papers on The Science of Administration* (New York: Institute on Public Administration, 1937). The integration of politics and administration has generated an even more extensive literature. Harold Stein's *Public Administration and Policy Development* (New York: Harcourt Brace Jovanovich, Inc., 1952) represented the definitive casebook at the time when the politics of administration viewpoint was in its ascendency. Marshall and Gladys Dimock provide the best textbook treatment of this perspective on administration in their *Public Administration,* 3rd ed. (New York: Holt, Rinehart and Winston, Inc., 1964). The most penetrating analysis of the politics of administration is probably found in the many articles by Norton Long, the best of which have fortunately been collected in a single volume, *The Polity* (Chicago: Rand McNally and Company, 1962). The best analysis of the President as Chief Executive is provided by Richard Neustadt in *Presidential Power: The Politics of Leadership* (New York: John Wiley and Sons, Inc., 1960). The relationship between the president and his cabinet is described and analyzed in detail by Richard Fenno, *The President's Cabinet* (Cambridge, Mass.: Harvard University Press, 1959). The interesting role assumed by departmental assistant secretaries is presented by Dean Mann and Jameson Doig in their *The Assistant Secretaries* (Washington: The Brookings Institution, 1965). *The Open Society* (New York: Simon and Schuster, Inc., 1968) by Abba P. Schwartz provides a detailed, first-person account of one assistant secretary who became caught in the internal political thickets of the Department of State. The relationship of the top-level civil service officials, the bureau chiefs, to their administrative superiors and to Congress is described concisely by J. Leiper Freeman in his *The Political Process: Executive Bureau and Legislative Committee Relations,* rev. ed. (New York: Random House, Inc., 1965).

## CHAPTER III

"The Strategy of Games" focuses on the pattern of interaction of organized groups in our political system. The logical starting point for this overall view of politics is Earl Latham's classic, *The Group Basis of Politics* (Ithaca: Cornell University Press, 1952). Lester Milbrath, *Political Participation* (Chicago: Rand McNally and Company, 1965) and Angus Campbell, et al., *The American Voter* (New York: John Wiley and Sons, Inc., 1964) provide empirical data to support the pluralist-bargaining-incremental theories first advanced by Latham and later refined in the writings of Robert Dahl, Charles Lindblom, and David Braybrooke. The most significant books by these individuals are: Dahl and Lindblom, *Politics, Economics, and Welfare* (New York: Harper and Row, Publishers, 1953); Dahl, *A Preface to Democratic Theory* (Chicago: The University of Chicago Press, 1956); Lindblom and Braybrooke, *The Strategy of*

*Decision* (New York: The Free Press, 1963); Lindblom, *The Intelligence of Democracy* (New York: The Free Press, 1965); and Dahl, *Pluralist Democracy in the United States* (Chicago: Rand McNally and Company, 1967). A broad philosophical justification of the pluralist-bargaining-incremental viewpoint is provided by Paul Diesing in his *Reason in Society* (Urbana: The University of Illinois Press, 1962). The nature of this orientation as it is revealed in Congress has been recorded superbly (and approvingly) in Aaron Wildavsky's *The Politics of the Budgetary Process* (Boston: Little, Brown and Company, 1964).

## CHAPTER IV

Introductions to the planning-programming-budgeting system (PPBS) of the executive branch can be obtained from several sources. An extended series of documents, which examine PPBS in detail, has been prepared by the U. S. Senate Government Operations Subcommittee on National Security and International Operations. Most of the documents in this series were published between 1967 and 1969. The *Public Administration Review* has devoted two full issues to PPBS: "Planning-Programming-Budgeting System: A Symposium," (**26**, No. 4, December 1966), and, "Symposium on PPBS Reexamined," (**29**, No. 4, March-April 1969). Both issues contain excellent articles that are especially well-written for the reader seeking a general introduction to the topic. References to advanced studies of systems analysis and cost-benefit analysis can be noted in the footnotes of Chapter Four of this volume, and in the many footnotes of the articles in the two *Public Administration Review* issues cited above. The best single case study on the attempted application of systematic analysis to public policy decision-making is provided by Frederick Mosher and John Harr in their *Programming Systems and Foreign Affairs Leadership: An Attempted Innovation,* (New York: Oxford University Press, 1970). The political consequences of PPBS and systems analysis are examined mainly in various articles, some contained in the volumes cited above and others contained in Chapter Eight, "The Politics of Analysis," of Gawthrop's *The Administrative Process and Democratic Theory* (Boston: Houghton Mifflin Company, 1970).

## CHAPTER V

The literature on technological complexity and sociopolitical turbulence is relatively new but already extensive. A modest introduction is provided by Emmanuel Mesthene's *Technological Change* (Cambridge, Mass.: Harvard University Press, 1970). *The Politics of Ecosuicide* (New York: Holt, Rinehart and Winston, Inc., 1971) is a collection of articles, edited by Leslie L. Roos, Jr., that focus specifically on environmental turbulence. The growing complexity and scale of the sociopolitical role assumed by private corporations is described in detail by Richard J. Barber in his book, *The American Corporation* (New York: E. P. Dutton and Company, Inc., 1970). The technological turbulence of the present and the future is examined in depth by Victor Ferkiss, *Technological Man: The Myth and The Reality* (New York: George Braziller, Inc., 1969); and Irene Traviss, ed., *The Computer Impact* (Englewood Cliffs, N. J.: Prentice-Hall, Inc., 1970). The sociopolitical and ethical aspects of environmental turbulence are explored in detail by Harvey Cox, *The Secular City* (New York: The Macmillan Company, 1965), Jacques Ellul, *The Technological Society*, (New York: Alfred A. Knopf, 1964), Michael Harrington, *The Accidental Century* (Baltimore: Penguin Books, 1965), Michael Crozier, *The Bureaucratic Phenomenon* (Chicago: The University of Chicago Press, 1964), and Theodore J. Lowi, *The End of Liberalism* (New York: W. W. Norton and Company, Inc., 1969).

## CHAPTER VI

As indicated in the text of this volume, one's view of the future, speculative though it may be, will influence one's perspective concerning the most appropriate role that public administration should assume in that perceived future. In this regard, more than enough imaginative insights concerning the state of the future are provided by Herman Kahn and Anthony Wiener in their very weighty volume, *The Year 2000: A Framework for Speculation on the Next Thirty-Three Years*, (New York: The Macmillan Company, 1967). A less overwhelming but equally stimulating source is *Toward The Year 2000: Work in Progress* (Daedalus, **96**, Summer 1967). Two other volumes which clearly imply the need for substantial administrative changes to meet demands of future technical and social change are John Kenneth Galbraith's *The New Industrial State* (Boston: Houghton Mifflin Company, 1967), and Warren Bennis and Philip Slater, *The Temporary Society* (New York: Harper and Row, Publishers, 1968). Also suggested are two well-written volumes which focus on the immediate future rather than on a distant date: Jean-Jacques Servan-Schreiber, *The Radical Alternative* (New York: W. W. Norton and Company, Inc., 1971) and Leonard Gross, *1985: An Argument For Man* (New York: W. W. Norton and Company, Inc., 1971). Administrative organization in response to rapid social change is examined in detail by Bertram Gross in his book *The Managing of Organizations: The Administrative Struggle* (New York: The Free Press, 1964). The role of public administration in a turbulent future is examined from several perspectives by a group of scholars in Frank Marini, ed., *Toward a New Public Administration* (San Francisco: Chandler Publishing Company, 1971). Public policy analysis and policy analysts of the future have been the main concern of Yehezkel Dror. His initial major effort in this regard is his excellent book, *Public Policymaking Reexamined* (San Francisco: Chandler Publishing Company, 1968). His subsequent efforts to build policy science into an intellectually meaningful and valid discipline are presented in an extended series of papers, reports, and monographs published by The Rand Corporation, Santa Monica, California. The relationship between environmental turbulence and established sociopolitical and ethical values is examined in detail in a volume of articles entitled *Values and the Future: The Impact of Technological Change on American Values* (New York: The Free Press, 1969), edited by Kurt Baier and Nicholas Rescher. For those interested in pursuing psychological humanism in greater depth, the works of Abraham Maslow provide a logical starting point. *Toward A Psychology of Being* (New York: D. Van Nostrand Company, 2nd ed., 1968) presents his theories formally. His *Eupsychian Management* (Homewood, Ill.: Richard D. Irwin, Inc., 1965) offers many stimulating ideas and hypotheses in a more informal, free-thinking journal. Such ideas and concepts as democratic participation in the decision-making process, agents of change, and matrix organizations are analyzed in detail in a special symposium issue of the *Public Administration Review* (**29**, No. 1, January-February 1969), entitled "Alienation, Decentralization, and Participation." Another issue of the same journal is devoted completely to the analysis of administrative planning and the future: "Changing Styles of Planning in Post-Industrial America," *Public Administration Review* (**31**, No. 3, May-June 1971). *Social Innovation in the City: New Enterprises for Community Development* (Cambridge, Mass.: Harvard University Press, 1969), edited by Richard S. Rosenbloom and Robin Morris, presents a series of working papers which examine the effects of technological, sociopolitical, and ethical change on urban life.

# Index